BACK UP NORTH

BACK UP NORTH

Ally Shepherd

Scratching Shed Publishing Ltd

Copyright © Ally Shepherd 2024
All rights reserved
The moral right of the authors has been asserted
First published by Scratching Shed Publishing Ltd in 2024
Registered in England & Wales No. 6588772
Registered office: 47 Street Lane, Leeds, West Yorkshire. LS8 1AP
www.scratchingshedpublishing.co.uk
ISBN 978-1068618994

Cover illustration: © Ally Shepherd
Back cover and interior images: © Ally Shepherd

No part of this book may be reproduced or transmitted in any form or by any other means without the written permission of the publisher, except by a reviewer who wishes to quote brief passages in connection with a review written for insertion in a magazine, newspaper or broadcast.

Every effort has been made to obtain the necessary permissions with reference to copyright material, both illustrative and quoted. We apologise for any omissions in this respect and will be pleased to make the appropriate acknowledgements in any future edition.

A catalogue record for this book is available from the British Library.

Printed and bound in the UK by

Unit 220, Fareham Reach, Fareham Road
Gosport, Hampshire, PO13 0FW

For my late grandmother, since it was one of her dusty old books that inspired the writing of this one. She made the best pies and was a formidable Scrabble opponent.

And to all my other ancestors, whose legacies of love and struggle I stand upon today.

Ally Shepherd was born and raised in the North of England though can often be found elsewhere, having lived in Europe, the Americas and Southeast Asia.
A teacher with a PhD in Education, in her spare time she enjoys salsa (both the food and the dance) and attempting to befriend passing animals.

Contents

Back Up North — xi

I.	Northern Granite: What Are Northerners?	1
II.	Black Diamonds and White Gold: A Brief History of the North	17
III.	Class and the Classroom: The North Today	33
IV.	God's Own Country: Northern Landscapes	57
V.	There's Nowt So Queer as Folk: Accent & Dialect	83
VI.	Gran's Scran: Food & Drink	101
VII.	A Northerner by Any Other Name: Immigration to the Region	119
VIII.	Good Morning, Mr Magpie! The Supernatural	139
IX.	We're All Mad Here: Northern Literature	153
X.	What's on t' Telly? Northern TV & Film	169
XI.	The North will Rise Again: Music from the North	189

Back Up North: A Reprise — 203
Other Claims to Fame — 205

References — 207

Acknowledgements

Thank you to family and friends who encouraged me, read my work, and whose humour has kept me laughing through the years.

I am also grateful to any beta readers who took the time to give feedback on my chapters, and to anyone I've quoted who kindly granted me permission to reproduce their words.

Lastly, my gratitude to any readers who have picked up this book. I appreciate you stopping by these pages.

Map* of the North

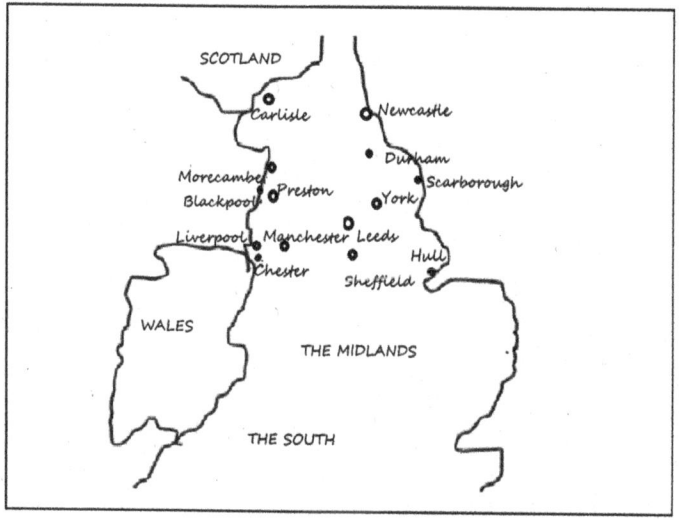

*I am using this term loosely as it is only vaguely accurate
(I apologise to Wales for deforming your beautiful coastline)

My North

My North is not smog and smoke
but green grass and open fields,
crags dotted with
kissing gates
and curious sheep.
My North is not coal mines and factories
but Morecambe Bay
and Pendle Hill
stretched out
at the top of the world.
Perhaps my North can be absurd
stood outside the club
at midnight
shivering in short skirts,
heels in hand.
Perhaps my North can be brash
scrapping outside the chippy
at dawn,
alcohol pulsing
through ardent veins.
But my North is not backwards,
        uneducated,
     uncivilised,
uncultured,
as the tired stereotype goes.
My North can be creative and crass
with the best humour I know,
friendly and quick to defend itself
from the brave souls
who might state otherwise.

Back Up North

"What d'ya wanna write a bloody book about the North for?"

The question comes from my dad as I'm sat in my parents' house during the first lockdown to stop the spread of Coronavirus. I'd spent the past ten years outside of not only the North but the whole of the UK, racking up a total of eight countries across five continents. Whilst I'd always returned home during holidays, it wasn't until international borders closed in March 2020 that I found myself back in the North for a prolonged period of time waiting out the plague – first from the safety of the roomy Cheshire countryside, and then from the cosmopolitan but Covid-infested Manchester.

My parents moved from Lancashire to Cheshire before I was born, so I grew up in a village just outside Chester. I spent an idyllic childhood playing out with friends, which usually involved giving each other seaties on our bikes to sit in a field eating 5p Freddos. Upon moving to the city's biggest high school full of hormonal time bombs, I adopted an appropriately teenage angst towards the world (by which I mean my hometown and the people in it but, at that time, that *was* my world). I was bored with the smallness and sameness of the place and the future on offer to me, so began plotting my escape. Once in sixth form, I took a General Studies class. It was mostly populated by kids who had chosen it as a doss elective, though I'd chosen it as an extra class as I loved learning (but had to keep it secret, as no-one liked a swat). Our balding teacher who looked like he'd lost the will to teach, several hundred apathetic students ago, played us a 1999 documentary about Cuban music called *Buena Vista Social Club*. It was bursting with an energy I had never heard or seen or touched before. I want to go there, I thought. I wanted to hear different music and meet different people and eat different food and see different places. I *will* go there, I resolved.

"I'm going travelling," I announced shortly afterwards to my parents, figuring I should inform them of my plans. After a pause in which they lowered their cigarettes, trying to ascertain the seriousness of my declaration, my dad spoke. "Well, we're not bloody paying for it."

"I never asked you to!" I hurled back, slamming the kitchen door and retreating to my bedroom.

I worked two jobs for six months in order to save enough money to spend the other half of the year in Latin America. I got hooked. I liked the newness, the excitement, the anonymity, the possibilities. After graduating from the University of Leeds, I trained as a teacher and, while everyone else I knew was getting married or having babies, I went overseas and didn't know when I'd be back.

I learned Spanish and how to make *pupusas*. I rode in the back of trucks and swam in old volcano craters. I also sweated (a lot) and got hounded by scorpions, snakes, and tarantulas. For the most part, I didn't get homesick. I did get tired of explaining that I was not from, nor had I ever lived in, London. I often had to explain that I wasn't Australian and that there were numerous people in the UK who didn't sound like Hugh Grant. On my travels from Madrid to Mandalay, I would occasionally stumble across fellow Northerners, gravitating towards their familiar accents, finding people who were up for a laugh and a pint. Whilst I'd set out to meet new people – *different* people – there was something comforting in wrapping myself in that memorable lilt and familiar habits. And despite how long I'd been away, there were still traces of the North in my voice, the words I used, the things that made me laugh, even my political views.

By the time the pandemic began, I was doing a PhD in the USA. Sat in my apartment in the snow-covered Midwest, I decided I didn't want to spend a lockdown of unknown length alone in a flat that had no balcony, let alone a garden to pace. I packed up a few things and flew back to hunker down with family in the Northwest for a month.

Then, it happened.

I saw the region with new eyes: the people, the community spirit, the humour. I felt safe and grateful and curious. Only by returning after so long away could I value its history and notice its secrets hidden in the architecture or in the turns of phrase heard at the bus stop.

Binge-watching TV during lockdown, I came across the 1972 film, *Home James*. In it, Yorkshire actor James Mason declared that he had very little affection for the area growing up and couldn't wait to get to London. In later life, however, he began returning for family reasons and grew more and more enthused for the region, making him "as bad as any other sort of convert". That is what happened to me: I became a born-again Northerner and, probably annoyingly, wanted to tell the world.

As I was broadcasting my newfound discovery, an American colleague asked me what a Northern worldview was, to explain the difference between the regions of England. I figuratively scratched my head, struggling to come up with an answer that didn't just rely on a few rubbish stereotypes. As a (sort of) academic who was a (sort of) sociologist, I'd spent years interested in other societies, cultures and identities. Now, I was asking the same questions of my own. What did it mean to be Northern? To have Lancastrian parents; to have grown up in Cheshire; to have spent formative years in Yorkshire; to be in Manchester at a time of crisis when it was demanding to be heard by Westminster? I wanted to understand myself by understanding my roots and, to do that, I had to understand the North.

I started with a dusty book from my late grandma's collection about old Lancashire traditions. It explained so many family quirks I'd previously seen as idiosyncratic, but now realised were cultural. I set out to read all the modern publications I could find about the North, devouring the varied answers to the question of what it meant to be Northern. Informative, hilarious, and inspiring, they allowed me to journey the region when restrictions meant we couldn't travel.

The only thing that niggled at me was that, since the 1950s, the non-fiction books about the North of England I could get my hands on were almost exclusively written by men. Some women told their stories through memoir, showing the political via the personal, though often contained to one locale. I was left wondering where women's voices were in mapping the North and its people on a broader scale. US writer Adrienne Rich declared that she believed "every woman's soul is haunted by the spirits of earlier women who fought for their unmet needs [and] those spirits dwell in us, trying to speak to us." Mine clamoured to be heard in the absence of such books, and so began my own response about the food and music, language and literature, working-class history and modern-day transformations, as well as natural and supernatural wonders.

Don't get me wrong – I love Brighton, have a childhood dream of going to Land's End (it sounds so romantic), and the capital is alright if your wallet has enough padding. But it's not the be-all and end-all of the UK.

If you're a Southerner poised to chuck this book in the bin thinking it's not for you, let me offer some reassurance. This narrative is not dedicated to trashing the South (though, fair warning, fun gets poked at Southerners and Northerners alike). Nor is this book a definitive list of Northernness – if such a thing can exist. Instead, it explores a curation of the history and land that makes its people so proud and me so happy to be back 'up North'. As pointed out by Lancashire writer Jeanette Winterson, everyone who tells a story tells it differently, to remind us we see life differently. As this is my subjective exploration of Northernness, I also include the disclaimer that my reflections don't cover every corner of the region. Thus, fellow Northerners, if you get to the end and rave that I've missed something proper Northern, please accept my apologies.

There is so much to make our broad chests puff out.

I. Northern Granite.

I am a Northerner by both nature and nurture. I did a DNA test for my thirtieth birthday, hoping to find some far-flung ancestry, but it fairly predictably declared that I was 81 per cent Northern (80 per cent of that Northwestern). The rest was Scottish and Irish, my dad's great-grandfather came down from the Highlands of Scotland, with one per cent Swedish (thanks to past invading Vikings, I assume). I managed to trace my family's marriage, birth, and death certificates back to the 1600s and it was pretty uniform: white, working-class Lancashire, with a couple of white, working-class Yorkshire folk thrown in for good measure. There were factory workers and beer sellers (no surprise there) and those who ended up in the Poor House, though one thing they all had in common was that their roots stretched down into Northern soils.

Both of my parents are from Lancashire – dad from the city of Preston, mum from Rossendale Valley – and my sister and I grew up in Cheshire, the 'posh' part of the Northwest where footballers reside. I used to insist that my hometown of Chester wasn't that posh though, because we didn't have a Waitrose. Then we got a Waitrose.

But before I get ahead of myself laying down my Northern credentials, I'll explain what Northerners are, in case it's unclear. I once had a colleague from London whose dad was from the Midlands (for many Londoners, anything north of the M25 is 'the North') whose mum used to tell her to roll up the car windows as they left London to visit family, warning that dragons lived in the North. That would be pretty interesting but, sadly, is not the case. The largest wing-ed thing we have is the sixty-six-foot steel Angel of The North, a tribute to the Northeastern coal miners of yesteryear which can be found watching over Gateshead.

So, what do we mean when we say 'the North'? According to author Stuart Maconie when writing about the North, for god's sake don't try to define it. London writer Charles Jennings believed it to start in Birmingham due to its tradition of metal bashing, but us Northerners know that Brummies are Midlanders. I reckon Cumbrian writer, Melvyn Bragg, did a good job of defining the region in his podcast *The Matter of the North*, starting at Hadrian's Wall in the west, extending down to the Dee estuary, moving over to the Humber, then back up the east coast. So, I wondered what the problem was until I stumbled across a number of issues.

Whilst chatting with two of my friends from university– a Sheffielder living in London and a Londoner married to a Northerner – I asked where in the North the latter's significant other was from. When she replied "Scunthorpe, Lincolnshire", I protested that Lincolnshire was the Midlands. She pulled up a map of England and pointed out that Scunthorpe sat geographically further north than both Sheffield and Chester. All parties perplexed, she shouted through the house to her partner who, defensively, insisted he was Northern and emphasised he was from North Lincolnshire. Turns out that despite being administratively under Lincolnshire, the area had become part of Yorkshire and the Humber in 1974's executive game of musical counties.

Later, the Sheffielder reminded me not to forget Bakewell tarts when writing about Northern food. "Isn't Bakewell near Buxton?" I asked, breaking the news that Buxton is in the Midlands, to which she protested that it is only thirty minutes from her house.

On the subject of Sheffield, Maconie's book, *Pies and Prejudice,* points out that the south of that city is pretty much in Derbyshire so Geordies regard it as the Midlands, though he goes on to defend the place since it grew rich on coal and steel, assuredly Northern industries. Northern in-fighting even surfaced from Yorkshire actress Judi Dench who once declared that Liverpool wasn't the North as it's "halfway up." The final Northern scuffle occurred when my own mum asked me if I would ever live "Up North" to which I replied: "Well, where are we now?!" Apparently to a Lancashire lass, Cheshire "doesn't count" as the North. Well, Northwestern-raised journalist Paul Morley (who wrote his own lengthy book called *The North*) gave us the honour of claiming that it begins in the Cheshire Plain. It may be close to the Midlands, but it's still the North. We're ten minutes from Wales but I'm not Welsh. In retrospect, I should have found a Geordie to declare that Lancashire wasn't the "real" North. Or better yet, a Scot who could slap their knee at the lot of us.

Assuming we have now established a rough geographical idea of what I'm referring to as 'the North', so what? Is the North-South divide arbitrary? Some argue that it is equal parts myth and material reality. Tyke poet and, since 2019, Laureate Simon Armitage in *All Points North* argued the former saying the North was too diverse to name as a whole, whereas Jennings proposed the latter in his book, *Up North*, claiming it is a fact of English life. He also opined that Northernness is often characterised by ugliness, poverty, and classlessness, to which the Mayor of Grimsby allegedly told him he should have stayed under his duvet down south. US writer and honorary Yorkshireman for a couple of decades, Bill Bryson, spoke of the North feeling like a different country in his book *Notes from a Small Island*; from how it looks and feels with its open moors and skies, mill towns, and stone villages, to the accents and dialects and directness of speech.

This sense of entering a different country may have something to it; we were a separate kingdom until the end of the tenth century. The loss of our independence has resulted in some centuries-long hangover as there have even been rumblings in favour of Yorkshire devolution. Can you imagine? The United Kingdom of England, Northern Ireland, Scotland, Wales, and Yorkshire. To be fair, its five million inhabitants outweigh those of Northern Ireland and are around the same in number as Scotland. During Scotland's 2014 independence referendum, jokes circulated begging Scotland to take 'us' with them, as many felt more in common with the Scots than with those down in Westminster.

It wasn't until I went to university in Yorkshire that I made the discovery that I was Northern. "Eeh, going t' other side o' t' Pennines," my Lancashire relatives teased, referencing the long-ended War of the Roses which pitted the House of York against the House of Lancaster (providing inspiration for the much-loved show, *Game of Thrones*). The University of Leeds campus I inhabited was populated by various Southerners, lamenting that London was better and laughing at how people sounded *Oop North*. I didn't however hear them complaining about our cheap pints – you just have to breathe in London and be charged a tenner. I quickly found a student from Sheffield and we banded together in our defensive Northern pride. After graduation she moved to London and has been there for ten years and decided that the capital is 'better', though I forgive her. She is not the only Northerner drawn in by London's pull of economic opportunities; two of my other Northern mates migrated south, though a few years later they both left. They lamented that it was hard to make friends in the capital and they missed Northern humour.

On discovering I was Northern, I asked my parents about the North-South divide and they told me that Southerners call us "Northern monkeys", due to being uncultured and uncivilised, and that we retaliate by deeming them "Southern fairies", as they don't know what hard work is and are unable to hold their drink. These mutually traded insults were news to me. Uncultured? Liverpool won the European Capital of Culture award in 2008 and we've given the world The Beatles, *Alice's Adventures in Wonderland* and chips, cheese and gravy.

As far back as the twelfth century, people have been documented talking of "northern granite" versus "southern softies". George Orwell wrote in *The Road to Wigan Pier* in 1937, "when you go to the industrial North you are conscious, quite apart from the unfamiliar scenery, of entering a strange country. This is partly because of certain real differences which do exist, but still more because of the North-South antithesis which has been rubbed into us for such a long time past. There exists in England a curious cult of Northernness, a sort of Northern snobbishness. A Yorkshireman in the South will always take care to let you know that he regards you as inferior. If you ask him why, he will explain that it is only in the North that life is 'real' life, that the industrial work in the North is the only 'real' work, that the North is inhabited by 'real' people, the South merely by rentiers and their parasites. The Northerner has 'grit', he is grim, 'dour', plucky, warm-hearted and democratic; the Southerner is snobbish, effeminate and lazy – that at any rate is the theory."

Fast-forward to the twenty-first century where academics Alan Hughes and Peter Atkinson from the University of Central Lancashire found that even today Southerners view

Northerners as insensitive and unsophisticated, while Northerners see Southerners as privileged and unfriendly compared with themselves as friendly and practical.

Having been out of the country for the best part of a decade, I wondered if such divided opinions were still held by your average Brit. Had the North and South since embraced one another in Brexit-inspired nationalism? To test this theory, I asked a number of people in a very unofficial survey – Northern and otherwise – how they would describe us. Without a doubt, the number one answer was friendly, followed by funny, more community-minded and family-oriented, chatty, warm, unaffected, outgoing, "can take the piss out of themselves", and "like a drink." At which another added: "It's the beer. Up North it's proper beer. Down South it's all warm weak London beer." I was also told: "Gobby and loud with annoying accents" (from a Southerner, if you hadn't guessed). As well as: "they have weird names for meal times and they have several different types of weird names for bread." More specifically, a friend's sister reflected that "it's hard for Northerners to reconcile themselves to the cost of the cloakroom at a night club. So, we prefer to stand and freeze in the queue." Go out on any winter's night and you'll see Northern lasses in short skirts and backless tops, huddled together on the way to the club, 'beer jackets' and high spirits the only things keeping us warm as, god forbid, we pay a quid to avoid hypothermia. (Leeds band Kaiser Chiefs paint this vivid picture in their song 'I Predict a Riot'.)

On the point about being more community-oriented, to celebrate the anniversary of VE day in 2020, a member of my hometown's School of Performing Arts organised his entire street (think terraced red brick houses with geranium-potted front yards) to perform a physically distanced all-singing, all-dancing version of 'We'll Meet Again', complete with 1940s costumes. Just the uplift people needed during the height of the lockdown. In the *Lancashire Evening Post*'s 1971 publication *It's an Old Lancashire Custom*, journalist Sylvia Corbridge reckoned that Lancashire folk, whilst appreciating those who 'keep themselves to themselves', are genuinely good neighbours. "She adores talking over the back wall, popping in to borrow a knitting pattern, or making a bit of dinner for that poor old soul at No. 29 who's in bed with arthritis." I can confirm that these traditions continue up North as my dad is constantly chatting with neighbours on the front lawn or popping over to help someone with a garden project, and I took some homemade cordial to an elderly neighbour with Covid when news got round the street that he was ill.

At the start of the pandemic, my parents informed me their neighbours had been round to check on them, knowing they were self-isolating, and offered to do their shopping for them, and my sister told me her street had a WhatsApp group to look out for one another. When it was safe to do so, both sets of neighbours dragged foldup chairs into their respective cul-de-sacs and had a gathering. It reminded me about Northern villages: the lady in the post office knows your name and where you live; you stop and talk to your neighbours on your way out to the car to discuss the weather and catch up on the latest gossip; you say 'hi' to the couple whose children used to go to school with yours even if they are grown up now and you don't keep in touch.

Every time I fly into the UK via Manchester rather than London, I end up with someone's tale of where they've been and how they've been holidaying there since they were a kid and how "our James" is going to join them next year because the package deal was such good value for money as opposed to simply avoiding eye contact with one another while we shuffle through immigration or wait for our resuscitated plane food.

The *Guardian*'s North of England editor, Helen Pidd, (in a newspaper published in Manchester before it moved to

Fleet Street in 1961) argued that there's a persistent view amongst Londoners that the most intelligent folk from the North end up in the capital, like moths drawn to the bright lights of the city. On the topic Jennings explains that he, like all capital city residents, is "condescending and parochial", having no idea what's going on outside the city, though he admits he believes that "however rotten the metropolis becomes, it and all its related works are still superior to anywhere else." My sister became animated upon hearing this claim, complaining that the people in the Southern office of her company are rude to people in the Northern one: "They think we are absolute hillbillies." Adding, "they also think we're pissheads." When I asked if I could quote her on that, she replied: "Ask me again tomorrow, I've had a few glasses of wine."

I thought the North was summed up quite nicely when, in 2021, a bunch of people got snowed into Tan Hill Inn, the highest pub in England in North Yorkshire, when they had gone to see an Oasis tribute band. These strangers ended up on international news – it made it into my local paper in Wisconsin – as they drank and ate their way through the storm, got T-shirts to commemorate the event, and arranged to do it again, minus snowstorm, the next year.

Caroline, a friend of mine with a Northern dad and a Southern mum, said Northerners are "tight". I asked her what she meant, and she said her dad was obsessed with turning the lights off to save money. My own dad, a perfectly Northern combination of comical and curmudgeonly, would often declare it was "like Blackpool Illuminations in here" when we left the lights on around the house. Or if I left the kitchen light on, en route to the lounge, he'd grumble: "There'll be bloody planes landing on t' lawn soon." He was the kind of dad who showed his love through 'fixing things' and providing for the family (amidst obligatory protestations of the rest of the family's ability to do anything the 'right' way). Whilst my mum thought money was there to be spent (preferably on shoes) and wanted to give us everything she hadn't had, my dad thought we should know what it was like to live without, and so minimal lights were allowed to be on at any one time in the house.

In keeping with our history of thrift, my maternal great-grandfather used to say: "Look after the pennies and the pounds take care of themselves" and, of course, "money doesn't grow on trees." They were two well-worn expressions in our household, cutting open toothpaste and suncream bottles a way to "get our money's worth". One day my dad's firefighter-cum-builder friend Lee (a fellow Lancastrian) was over for a barbeque and my mum teased him for never turning his heating on as he's too tight. "Careful," my dad said. At first, I thought he meant 'be careful or you'll get a clip round t' ear 'ole', but then realised he thought him not tight but careful with money. Lee explained: "It's a Lancashire thing", adding with a wink, "but were not as bad as Yorkshire." (Spoken like a true Lancastrian.)

On asking my dad about the perceived divide as he sat in 'his chair' reading the Sunday paper, he lowered the pages and ran his hand thoughtfully over a scalp that had long shed its hair, answering that Northerners were friendlier and "I suppose more working-class. There are more blue-collar jobs here." Then he added with a chuckle, "Southerners think we're all flat caps and whippets", referencing the stereotype of working-class Northerners and their keeping of whippets as race dogs instead of the more expensive greyhound. Considering there was a 2016 *Guardian* article titled 'More than flat caps and whippets: exhibition to celebrate the best of the north about an exposition at the Lowry,' I guess the stereotype lives on.

A US colleague's Southern husband, Nick, told me that

Northerners "present themselves as tougher, more hardy". As Maconie teased: "Some of the clichés about us are true. We are friendlier and more helpful. And if you don't agree, we might glass you." When I asked my auntie about Northerners, she replied simply, "tough as old boots" (perhaps not surprisingly, coming from a woman married to a man who'd spent a spell in the nick during his youth). Said uncle, who wouldn't look out of place in a Hell's Angels gang, covered in tattoos sporting a handlebar 'tash, was actually a big softie who constantly cracked dad jokes and play-fought with the dogs until his arms were all scratched up, canines delighted.

Dame Judi Dench, talking of the idea of a Northern hardiness, informed fans that she rarely complains. I feel this is a Northern attribute as my dad instilled in us the idea that going to the doctor is unnecessary, unless your arm is about to drop off, and we would instead be told to "buck up, there's nowt wrong wi' you" when we tried to get out of going to school. My maternal grandma, in-keeping with this hardy tradition and never one to complain, lived (unknowingly) with a dislocated shoulder for months until she ended up in hospital for something else and a nurse accidentally rammed it back in place helping her into bed.

Nick also said he thought of us as less welcoming to outsiders. Whilst his perception might seem true in comparison to multicultural London, the *Telegraph* reported in 2018 that visitors were actually more likely to get a smile and some friendliness in the North than in London or the Home Counties. According to a 2015 *Vice* article titled 'Southerners, Science Says you're Officially Not as Friendly as Northerners', this is because we have less traffic and are only ever ten yards from a chip shop. Said science emerged from a University of Cambridge study comprising four hundred thousand respondents, ranking Scots as the friendliest, suggesting that the further north you go, the nicer people get.

We are, then, left with a rather weird combination of "rough and smooth". As Simon Armitage pointed out, we might get a tattoo of our hometown but hide it from our mum, or say hi to anyone, but start a fight if they "look at us funny." In a 2019 BBC sketch, Manchester comedian Brennan Reece walks down a country lane arguing that "we don't care where you're from – if you're Polish or gay – we're friendly round here", at which point a driver rolls past shouting "get the fuck out the way". Our leading lad ends the video by nutting the Southern voiceover guy who dared slag off the North. But we're dead friendly, honest.

A Southerner who preferred to remain nameless reckoned we "take the piss out of everything" and have a "sense of humour about serious stuff to cheer people up." Bill Bryson said that, even after twenty years in the North, he was constantly amazed and impressed by the quality of humour you find in the most unlikely places – "places where it would simply not exist in other countries." One example of this that recently made me chuckle was a bench spotted in Darwen reading:

> *Nellie & Norman Bentley*
> *Reunited Once Again In Heaven*
> *He'll Not Be Appy Bout That*

My mate, Rach, who I've known through home bowl haircuts (hers) and goth phases (mine), agrees with this assessment of our humour, offering a story of how, when working in a hospital during the pandemic, a fellow midwife offered her a biscuit. Rach recoiled, concerned about the virus, though her colleague just chortled and pointed out that the clinic was probably already riddled with the stuff so they might as well enjoy a biscuit to dunk in their brew. Northern women getting on with things despite adversity, humour intact.

The Northern men I spoke to almost always mentioned

sports. As a lad, my dad played amateur rugby for Blackburn then, of course, there's the footie. My mum used to say one of the reasons she married my dad was because he didn't like football. Then he retired and started watching it, though she hasn't divorced him yet. Thanks to trade union campaigns for a two-day weekend, the industrial working-class were given Saturdays to have a kickabout (Sundays were still reserved for church), thus beginning a Northern obsession. In W.R. Mitchell's *Lancashire Mill Town Traditions*, a Bolton spinner declared that "it was a matter of pride to be well-dressed at weekends. A man always had to have money for a packet of cigarettes, a pint of beer and to let him watch Bolton Wanderers play football on a Saturday afternoon."

For Cestrians, whose local team have not yet burst into the big leagues, many support Liverpool or Manchester United. In primary school, my allegiance flip flopped back and forth depending on who my friends supported until I realised that I didn't care and my days of trying to learn the players' names became a thing of the past. I do, however, use Man U's worldwide fame to my advantage as, living abroad, I gave up saying I was from Chester as no-one has ever heard of it, instead telling people I'm from Manchester (close enough in name and geography). In 2023, I was invited to Thanksgiving dinner with a friend's family and got excited when a guest told me he had visited Manchester, rather than the usual "we went to London to see Buckingham Palace". My excitement was soon quashed though, as he proceeded to describe going to a pub "with real blue-collar workers" like it was a safari to observe Northerners in their natural, impoverished habitats.

From my less-than-scientifically-rigorous poll, it seems like the invisible but lingering North-South divide stands firm. We could argue, though, that differences are simply used for some good old British banter. Our crap weather has inspired old sayings such as: "Three ills come out of the

North: a cold wind, a shrinking cloth, and a dissembling man" and the Devon proverb claiming that only "knaves and foul weather come out of the North." Granted, when you go to Manchester you have to carry an umbrella in your bag at all times; and when I moved to Leeds I had to invest in a 'gust-buster' brolly as the regular ones would quickly be turned inside out by the city's infamous wind. But all this talk of knaves and dissembling men is a bit unnecessary. As was Oxfordian novelist Martin Amis claiming that "England is a one-city nation. I get the horrors when I go to provincial England. The sort of trundling, pottering English – I can't be doing with that". Well, we can't be doing with the likes of folks thinking like that.

Despite my defensiveness, the judgments flow both ways. In the 1950s, Sylvia Corbridge contended that "we have always believed, for instance, that south of the Trent nobody speaks to the folk next door. 'They don't bother with their neighbours,' we sniff and proceed to describe, with pursed lips, the loneliness of Cousin Sarah who moved from Blackburn to Bayswater and never had the opportunity to say more than 'Good morning' to the woman next door before returning, broken-hearted and lonely, back north."

As well as a Northern pride, there exist strong regional and local identities, which are not necessarily mutually exclusive. These feelings of belonging can be held at the same time, as a friend of a friend told me: "I'm incredibly proud to be Northern and incredibly proud to be Mancunian." On the other hand, competing identities can pit one part of the North against another, as with Lancashire and Yorkshire who still like to wield their historical grudges. According to Charles Jennings, geography is to blame for some differences, as Yorkshire folk get the North Sea wind across the moors whereas Lancastrians get the damp draughts of the Atlantic which, he argued, gives them a "moist, bedewed view of the world which translates into humour, whimsy, and song." Then, as if he felt he'd been too generous to the Northern region, he added that, for Lowry, it also translated into atrocious paintings.

Fighting in the Northwest corner, Manchester and Liverpool are in a constant state of rivalry, and the Northeast's Newcastle and Sunderland have been bickering since the English Civil War, with football a common channel for these historical wall-pissing contests to manifest. In 1974, when regional boundaries were redrawn across the North, battle lines were also drawn. Greater Manchester and Merseyside grew up and flew the nest, while parts of Yorkshire, Lancashire, Cheshire, and Cumbria played pass the parcel with their unsuspecting border towns. Rumour has it that one along the Lancashire-Yorkshire border woke up the next day with what looked like a bullet hole in its new sign. A conflict began between the council and the locals, the latter outraged at having been given over to the enemy. So, you see, it's complex. We project a united front to rally against a discerning South but, behind closed moors, we scratch and scrape amongst ourselves (with Yorkshire occasionally trying to ditch the rest of us entirely).

So what of this Northern worldview I promised my colleague? Others have tried to summarise it, with Paul Morley writing about the multitude of things that begin in the North – from fights and journeys to rivers and spells; and Simon Armitage arguing that it means more than women wearing aprons and hair rollers whilst scrubbing the front step, or daughters in supermarket jeans eating baked beans out of a can. Stuart Maconie expanded on Northernness as philosophical rather than simply geographical: "It's about appreciating that an afternoon's snow is an excuse for sledging, not a state of emergency. It's about realising that the best place to drive a Range Rover is Cumbria not Islington.

It's about embracing that life is short and work is hard and that London is not the answer to everything."

Northernness lives in both the political and in the mundane. It's as significant as the former kingdom's struggle to retain its own identity apart from that of the dominant South; it's solidarity in the face of adversity, with a long history of anti-establishment struggles. It's as trivial as knowing what someone means when they mention 'that house in the middle of the M62'. It's down-to-earth and fun-loving and can often be found at the pub drinking a pint. It's having a 'going out' coat and keeping the 'best plates' for a special occasion, with no event short of a member of the Royal Family popping over for a crumpet a good enough reason for your nan to get them out of the cabinet. As Melvyn Bragg has stated: "If you're born in the North or brought up in the North, it never leaves you. It's your place... your first world."

The last comment I received was from a former colleague of mine who, when asked what her stereotypes were of Northerners, replied: "Wait... people live north of London?! Are they okay?" I will now dig into some of our historical and modern-day triumphs, trials, and tribulations, and you can make your own mind up on the matter.

II. Black Diamonds and White Gold

Spanish-American philosopher Jorge Santayana once said that "history is a pack of lies about events that never happened by people who weren't there." Well, I wasn't there during the following events I describe, but am pretty sure they did happen. Not that you'd necessarily know it, as some have been consigned to the history bin labelled 'do not open' and buried on Riggs Moors for no one ever to find. (Said moor, in the Yorkshire Dales National Park, is the most remote place in England, as measured by distance to the nearest road.) Whilst Santayana may have been talking about History with a capital 'H', I agree with Accrington's Jeanette Winterson who argued that we are all historians in our small way. So to delve deeper into understanding the North, I wanted to look at how it came about, not just what it's up to nowadays.

Our past has shaped our present, from gaining wealth from cotton and coal to (ongoing) working-class struggles for the pound cake to be sliced more equally. This working-class history can be seen in well-known works of literature such as Charles Dickens's *Hard Times*, Elizabeth Gaskill's *North and South*, and George Orwell's *Road to Wigan Pier*. But perhaps it's best to begin with a notable incident of class struggle from the history books: the 1819 bloodshed at St Peter's Field, Manchester. Sixty thousand people had peacefully gathered to call for the vote to be extended to all men (women weren't getting a look in for another hundred years) when the military charged at the crowd killing men, women, and even a child, leaving fifteen dead and hundreds more injured. The violent event earned the nickname of the Peterloo Massacre, after the earlier Battle of Waterloo in 1815. Manchester City Council has a memorial to the event consisting of concentric stone circles engraved with the names of the victims, unveiled in 2019 on the two hundredth anniversary. Percy Bysshe Shelley, Sussex-born poet and husband of *Frankenstein* author Mary Shelley, wrote a response to the Peterloo Massacre titled *Masque of Anarchy*, a kind of call to arms for the masses.

Rise like Lions after slumber
In unvanquishable number –
Shake your chains to earth like dew
Which in sleep has fallen on you –
Ye are many – they are few.

Not long after the massacre, a group emerged called the Chartists. They represented the first mass movement driven by the British working-class, beginning in 1832, with four hundred branches and 50,000 members by 1842. They wanted suffrage for all men, not just voting rights for property-owners.

Moreover, they were angry that industrialisation had replaced once respected weavers with machinery that undervalued the skilled artisan, converting people into expendable machine operators in places around the country such as Bradford. Their newspaper was called *The Northern Star* and mass meetings were held across the North as well as in Birmingham and Glasgow. Despite their People's Charter, strikes, and mass petitions signed by millions, they didn't immediately win any of their demands; riots were quashed, leaders imprisoned. One of the leaders was William Cuffay, a tailor born to a white English mother and black African father who had met on a naval ship where his mother was a cook and his father, formerly enslaved, worked. Cuffay, who had lost his job after a tailors' strike, began to organise in London for universal suffrage. In 1848, he was sentenced and sent to Tasmania on charges of organising an uprising against the government. Despite such setbacks, a series of reforms expanding the vote to more and more men were established over the following decades, and now their original demands form part of the building blocks of our current democracy that we may take for granted.

In 1903, Manchester's Emmeline Pankhurst was one of a group of women who believed that they should be able to vote too. With this in mind, they created the Women's Social and Political Union dedicated to "deeds not words". Pankhurst was born to politically active middle-class parents in Moss Side and married to one of the founding members of Manchester's Liberal Association. She became one of the leaders of the women's suffragette movement alongside Northumberland's Emily Davison from Morpeth, who famously threw herself in front of the King's Horse in 1913, resulting in her death. (Incidentally and perhaps prophetically, Morpeth means 'murder path' in Old English). Before being martyred for the cause, Davison had been arrested nine times and on hunger strike seven, having to be constantly force fed, so she was no stranger to extreme action. Other lesser-known Northern women leading the suffragette movement include Prestonian Teresa Billington-Greig, who was the founder of the Women's Freedom League and wrote *The Militant Suffrage Movement* in 1911 and *The Consumer in Revolt* in 1912, linking consumerism and feminism, showing her to be a woman ahead of her time.

By 1917, all men over twenty-one had the vote, thanks to some eccentric post-war thinking along the lines of: if they can die for their country, they can vote for their leaders. Then followed women over thirty with property or with propertied husbands, which included two thirds of women over the age of twenty-one. Finally, in 1928 – the year my maternal grandmother was born – all women over twenty-one were granted the vote.

Industrialisation, the process which – for better or worse – puffed out the world as we now know it, was birthed in the North of England in the eighteenth century. It was during this time that the first canal was built in 1791. Bridgewater Canal was named after the Duke of Bridgewater, who owned coal mines in the North and wanted a way of transporting the so-called 'black diamond' around rapidly industrialising Manchester. Not long afterwards, others followed suit during a period creatively named 'canal mania', revolutionising transportation across the country. Not everyone was pleased with these changes, though. The North's anti-establishment spirit reared up in resistance to inventions that would put many people out of work. In 1812, the Luddites – a group founded in Nottingham opposing the trend – had a literal bash at stopping the onward march of industrialisation by trashing West Yorkshire textile mills. They failed in their mission to stop the onward march of technology and were mostly either executed or sent to Australia.

Of those embracing change, twenty-eight textile workers founded the Rochdale Society of Equitable Pioneers in 1844, forming a basis for the modern co-operative movement. Proponents of co-operatives argue they are democratic, value-oriented groups that circulate money within communities rather than the pockets of the already wealthy where benefits often fail to 'trickle down' to the masses. In 1863, many co-operatives in the North amalgamated and based themselves in Manchester, where they continue to exist as The Co-operative Group today. Others, unsatisfied with their lot in industrial England, left in search of riches in the USA or Australia. Between 1830 and 1930 one million people passed through Liverpool's port in search of the New World. Others stopped at the port after finding work there, joining the multicultural area full of Irish fleeing the potato famine, Caribbean workers, and Chinese sailors. Villages across the North became sprawling communities in which new factories and homes were "tastelessly intermingled, bound together by soot", according to Northern writer W.R. Mitchell.

A German named Friedrich Engels wrote of Manchester (at the time nicknamed 'Cottonopolis') in his 1844 book *The Condition of the Working Classes in England*: "the races that live in these ruinous cottages... must have really reached the lowest stage of humanity" as unsanitary conditions led to epidemics of diseases which killed as many as 4,000 people on Oldham Road alone. Anita Street in Manchester, as it has been known since the 1960s, was originally named Sanitary Street after houses were eventually built with their own sinks and toilets to address this issue of unsanitary overcrowding in the back-to-back slum housing. The modern residents disliked the associations and knocked off some letters on either side to give it the current name it bears today.

Engels met his fellow countryman Karl Marx (who, according to Stuart Maconie, was "a bit of a lardarse with rubbish hair who nicked all of Friedrich's ideas") in a Manchester library and history was made as the Communist Manifesto became a call to arms to liberate the sorry labourers as workers of the world were implored to unite and seize the means of production. The workers indeed united in riots in 1862 as people became increasingly dissatisfied with their positions in newly industrialised Britain, with many mothers working right up to birth (infant mortality was unsurprisingly high), and mill workers having fluff-filled lungs from a practice called 'kissing the shuttle' in which they had to suck the thread through a hole.

My own family tree is peppered with factory workers. My great auntie worked in a shoe factory all her life, a tiny woman with a vice-like grip who never had kids and got herself a pixie haircut when ten-year-old me asked why all old women have perms. Her husband was secretary of the fire brigade's union in Lancashire and involved in Labour Party politics (and, briefly, with the Communist Party) who insisted on greeting with a kiss on the lips, though I noticed male family members weren't offered the same privilege. My other great uncle, Joe, worked at a factory his entire life, losing a finger in the process. His cotton weaving wife Lily (who drove ambulances during the Second World War) also worked at a mill with my grandma before both left; the latter decided that fluffing people's hair afforded better working conditions than fluffing her own lungs; the former became a cleaner for a mill owning couple, much to my mum's delight as she got their girls' expensive clothing hand-me-downs.

We also can't talk about industrialisation without acknowledging the link between the transatlantic slave trade and the rise of the Northwest. In his book *It Happened in Lancashire* (Lancashire originally including Merseyside and Greater Manchester), Malcolm Greenhalgh states that the county used to be "one of the poorest parts of Britain due to its difficult terrain, poor soil, estuaries and bogs, but it went on to become one of the wealthiest through coal, cotton and slavery." He describes how the first ships left Liverpool in 1700 and from then, eight-hundred-and-seventy-eight trips were made with clothing and other manufactured goods exchanged for cargos of enslaved people from West and

Central Africa who were made to work in the West Indies and southern states of the USA. The ships returned to Lancashire with rum, cane sugar, and cotton.

During the height of the British empire, Liverpool was the third richest city after London and Glasgow and is home to the highest number of listed buildings outside the capital. Their origins are visually and vividly displayed in the International Slavery Museum, home to one installation that stands out in my mind: a map of the city. A friend and I once had an educational but gloomy day out of going to watch the newly released film *Twelve Years a Slave* followed by a visit to the museum. At the click of a button, you can see all the beautiful buildings constructed with money earned from the labour of enslaved Africans. Another example of visual storytelling can be seen in Lagos-born and Gateshead-bred historian David Olusoga's BBC series *A House Through Time*. It focuses on a house and its accompanying history, one such being a terraced town house on Liverpool's Faulkner Street. One of its occupants who'd benefitted from the slave trade went from riches to rags as the cotton market crashed, moved to New York to re-establish himself on Wall Street and, in an ironic twist of fate, was drafted to fight in the US civil war on the side of the Union.

At its height, cotton money sustained palatial homes in Cumbria and North Lancashire. More recently, the National Trust updated information on its properties listing connections to money gained from the slave trade, which included Hare Hall in Macclesfield and Quarry Bank Mill in Wilmslow. We could consider following in the footsteps of Glasgow University by paying reparations for the ravages of our global ladder-climbing when, in 2019, they pledged £20 million to the University of the West Indies for a Development Centre. Better late than never.

The 2021 book, *African Lives in Northern England: From*

Roman Times to the 21st Century, documents the people who have been in the North for longer than we may think. However, unlike the Americas, enslaved people did not extensively labour in the UK, though some traders brought servants home with them. At Sunderland Point, seven miles from Lancaster, you can find 'Sambo's Grave', commemorating the death of a young, enslaved boy in 1736 who was brought to live with a trader. Some say he died of homesickness, others that he got measles. There can be read prose not unlike Martin Luther King Jr's renowned dream: "The GREAT JUDGE his Approbation founds / Not on a Man's COLOUR, but his WORTH OF HEART" (a bit paradoxical under the circumstances, but touching nonetheless). The grave to this day bears flowers or stones painted by local children.

The interconnectedness of the slave trade and the Northwest was starkly demonstrated during the Lancashire Cotton Famine in the nineteenth century. By 1825, cotton was Britain's biggest import and Lancashire was the driving force, its family-based weaving and spinning cottage industry replaced by factories, heralding the dawn of the Industrial Revolution. However, by 1861 as a result of the US civil war (another infamous North-South divide) cotton shipments were stopped while the future rights of enslaved people were fought out and, on this side of the pond, the working-class people of Lancashire felt the effects. Families who depended on the work in the cotton mills – which could be mum, dad, and the kids with their nimble little fingers – suddenly had no income and the ensuing poverty meant that people didn't have enough to eat. Soup kitchens were opened in 1862 but some people refused help, even as their children starved. "Just give us a job", they'd appeal, a prime example of 'Lancashire pride'.

While UK traders generally supported the continuation of slavery to protect their livelihoods, the workers of Manchester did not. On December 31, cotton workers met in Manchester and agreed to support the fight to end slavery. This display of solidarity was directly addressed by US President Abraham Lincoln in a letter "to the working men of Manchester" for their "sublime Christian heroism, which has not been surpassed in any age or in any country." Slavery was abolished in 1865 in the US, but it wasn't until 1883 that a law passed through the House of Commons to end slavery across the British Empire. William Wilberforce, a Northern man from Hull, is known for being at the forefront of the abolition movement among British politicians. He credited his religious beliefs as pushing him towards social reform – firstly for enslaved peoples abroad and later for the working-class at home. In the 2006 film addressing his activism, *Amazing Grace*, his colleague Thomas Clarkson speaks of such a revolution, linking the fight for freedom for enslaved people working in American fields to the fight for freedom for the workers in English factories and mines, asking if they shouldn't be free to prosper also? Of course, the abolition movement was also fought by activists of colour across the world in various ways, one famous example being the Haitian Revolution where slaves revolted against the French in 1791 resulting in independence in 1804; and there were countless other smaller rebellions throughout the Americas during the seventeenth, eighteenth, and nineteenth centuries. In the US alone, there were at least two hundred and fifty documented uprisings of ten or more people.

Some say that history is an early warning system and, as we saw in 2020, people are still struggling for racial justice in the present day. That year saw Black Lives Matter protests, triggered by a video recording of the death of a black man at the hands of a white policeman in Minneapolis, USA. Outrage and support for the movement rippled out across the country in the largest protests since the Civil Rights Movement of the 1960s, and then to dozens of other countries across the world. Here in the UK, Bristol protesters toppled a statue of Tory MP and slave trader Edward Colston and rolled him through town and into the canal. (Shortly after, Google Maps was updated to show him located in the middle of the water.) Various other statues and street names celebrating slave traders were identified across the country, with London mayor Sadiq Khan pledging to rename a number of streets, and a statue of slaveholder Robert Milligan was formally removed from outside the Museum of London Docklands.

Unbeknown to me, my own city had a statue commemorating Field Marshal Stapleton Cotton for his achievements as a cavalry officer. He was also a slave owner who received compensation upon the abolition of the slave trade, lest he be inconvenienced. Predictably, a bunch of people who likewise had never given the statue a second glance before then came out of the woodwork to bemoan its potential removal. Other statues that came under overdue scrutiny included Dunham Massey stately home, which had a statue of a kneeling black servant, since deemed inappropriate and removed, as well as Manchester's Piccadilly Gardens statue of Robert Peel, Bury-born Conservative Prime Minister and founder of the Metropolitan Police, who opposed abolition on the grounds that it would harm the cotton industry. Peel also stands in Woodhouse Moor in Leeds, as well as London and Glasgow, revered across the country it seems. In a strange development in Newcastle, counter-protesters went to defend Prime Minister Earl Grey's statue, despite the fact that he was Prime Minister when slavery was abolished and not on the Black Lives topple list.

To those defending the silhouettes of the white men of yesteryear, I'd argue that removing statues is not an erasure of history since the main purpose of statues is not to teach, but to celebrate. And I can think of a whole host of better people we could celebrate in metal form instead, for example, those who fought to expand human rights, not take them away. And if we insist on celebrating violence, we could do as the Swedish did in commemorating the moment that a middle-aged woman whacked a marching neo-Nazi in the back of his head with her handbag. She became a local hero and can now be found, forever poised in action, in the plaza in Varberg.

Other ideas we could celebrate might include the introduction of the beginnings of a Welfare State in 1906 which aimed to address some of the inequalities expressed by Will Crooks, a Labour MP who said in 1908: "Here in a country rich beyond description, there are people poor beyond description." During the Boer War, two thirds of Manchester volunteers were rejected on the grounds of being too unfit to join and Lancashire soldiers during the First World War were known for being the smallest. The end of the war brought economic difficulty and in 1929, during the time of a general strike, soup kitchens were common. One man using them claimed that "it's nobbut t' poor as helps t' poor" with kind families making broth and butchers donating cheap offal. If it came to eating or keeping warm, keeping warm was chosen with some families breaking up furniture to make fire.

In 1937, acclaimed writer George Orwell was tasked with going to the North to write about the "condition of England" in his controversial (and sometimes contradictory) book *The Road to Wigan Pier*. His often-unflattering prose details the poverty and hardships faced by the Northern mining communities, stating that "it's a kind of duty to see and smell such places now and again, especially smell them, lest you should forget they exist; though perhaps it is better not to stay there too long." The places he was talking about were the industrialised areas with their "monstrous scenery of slagheaps, chimneys, piled scrap-iron, foul canals, paths of cindery mud criss-crossed by the prints of clogs", claiming that Sheffield "could justly be claimed to be the ugliest town in the Old World."

Orwell does, however, tip his gentleman's hat to the people working in the mines. He visits some, painting a hellish picture, arguing that "all of us really owe the comparative decency of our lives to poor drudges underground, blackened to the eyes, with their throats full of coal dust, driving their shovels forward with arms and belly muscles of steel." He also documents the various accidents and deaths occurring due to falling rock and not-so-controlled explosions. While to some younger readers this may seem like ancient history, one of my parents' friends lost his dad down a coal mine when he was four years old, so the effects are still in living memory. Orwell's description may have held some truth but may also have made some Northerners defensive since Orwell was, after all, an Eton-educated Southerner. Despite his opening chapter which paints a disdainful picture of the people in the boarding house he stayed in, he did repeat his admiration for Northern workers and used it as a springboard to promote a socialist agenda.

The arrival of the Second World War meant that Northern factories were called upon to belt out the necessary tools of warfare. Many women also went to work, landing them as fellow breadwinners, chipping away at entrenched British gender roles. For example, Preston women not in employment volunteered day and night to serve free refreshments to the service men and women using money raised locally. Records show that over fourteen million cups of tea and coffee were poured on dimly lit train stations as workers went to jobs on land, sea, and air. The effects of the Second World War nudged along the development of the Welfare State with the creation of the National Fire Service in

1941, universal education in 1944, and universal healthcare in 1948, with Park Hospital in Manchester known as being the 'birthplace of the NHS'. As someone who has lived and been unwell in the US, I can tell you how much we should appreciate free healthcare. (Having potentially rabid bats in my apartment set me back two thousand dollars as I needed to make sure I didn't die foaming at the mouth and trying to bite people like Cujo.)

Or we could celebrate 'battleaxe' women, those great British matriarchs common across the North, arms folded across ample bosom, busy putting people in their place. Leeds playwright, Alan Bennett, spoke of the Yorkshire tradition of women ruling the roost, adding that he wished they would rule it a bit more today. An article in *The Guardian* similarly lamented that nowadays fewer battleaxes exist, blaming effective contraception, with Lucy Mangan arguing that you can't sharpen neither tongue nor temper on just one or two children. Though if it's an either/or situation, I'll stick with the contraception, thanks. Going off Orwell's descriptions of the North's 'one up, one down' houses being filled by families of ten, you can see why birth control might be welcomed. Despite the hardships of providing for large families on small incomes, this poem shows a father's touching lament of the cost of another child on the way:

Tha'rt welcome, little bonny brid,
But shouldn't ha' come just when tha did,
Times are bad,
We're short o' pobbies for eawr Joe,
But that, of course, tha didn't know,
Did ta, lad?
But tho' we've a childer two or three,
We'll make a bit of reawm for thee;
Bless thee, lad,

Tha'rt th' prettiest brid we have i' th' nest.
So hutch up close to mi breast,
Awm thi dad.

My own dad grew up in the 1950s on a Preston estate. Once a wealthy market town, industrialisation saw thousands of workers arrive to live in the city, marking a period of pollution, poverty, and protests for the next hundred years. By the time my dad came along, manufacturing was in decline and rationing a hangover from the war. Three generations of family lived in their home, teenage siblings sharing rooms, grandparents' bed in the lounge. Three generations of our family continued to inhabit the house after this: my auntie and uncle, cousin and husband, their son, and a menagerie of pets including a one-eyed pug and a giant lizard.

I made my own entrance into the world in 1987, screaming, though my dad insists that was unrelated to the fact that this was the year Margaret Thatcher was re-elected for the third time. It made her the longest-running Prime Minister since Lord Liverpool (who was not, in fact, from Liverpool). From 1979, Margaret Thatcher's Conservative government put the wheels in motion for the de-industrialisation of the North and, despite the hardships of the industry, its workers didn't give it up without a fight. Mention Thatcher and someone will bring up the miner's strikes, led by Barnsley-born miner and Union leader Arthur Scargill. The strikes began the year my older sister was born in 1984 and lasted until the spring of 1985 in what has been described as the most bitter industrial dispute in British history, involving violent clashes between pickets and police. After losing as many as twenty-six million workdays, as counted per person, the strikes were deemed illegal and were defeated, spelling victory for the Tories and weakening trade union power.

According to Bill Bryson, if you divided the country in half from Bristol to the Wash (we can argue with him about that later) with roughly twenty-seven million people on each side, between 1980 and 1985 the South lost 103,600 jobs and the North 1,032,000. As is the subject of a number of Northern TV and film productions, these jobs losses caused devastation across many communities whose livelihoods depended on these now defunct industries. Although Maggie did trash the stereotype of women being the 'fairer' or 'weaker' sex, it's a shame that our first female PM claimed that there was no such thing as society and championed the individualistic political agenda we know all too well today.

With the days of the factories and coal mines gone, the issue is now one of a lack of jobs available in the areas that didn't experience a post-industrial renaissance. Poet Harry Man wrote of walking in downtown Middlesbrough past an old iron foundry, the remains of an "industrial Underworld, in which only the ghosts toil on." Writer Malcolm Greenhalgh explains: "King Cotton died a death in the 1950s and 1960s, King Coal in the 1970s and 1980s...The consequence is unemployment amongst the young of our Lancashire towns and cities; the army of NEETS – not in employment, education or training – for whom there is no job in t' mill or down t' pit." Mark Hodkinson similarly reflects that "despite poor conditions and low pay, the mills had provided social and structural identity and regular income. Rochdale is now post-recession, Anytown UK, devastated by the impact of the coronavirus pandemic... spotted with litter-strewn retail parks... The people are defeated."

That said, some believe that what the North lost in economic power, it gained in cultural growth (including in the New Labour years until the recession hit), which can perhaps be seen in numerous Northern areas winning City of Culture over the years, including Liverpool, Hull, and now

Bradford. But that doesn't help the former industrial towns whose teens may long to live in the cities looking for call centre jobs that don't quite hold the same sway as their industrial ancestors. Nor does it make up for the increase in inequality (according to the Gini coefficient, which measures household income distribution) during the Thatcher years which tells us what we may already know: that the dosh that was floating around at the time was not dished out evenly.

Jeanette Winterson argued that history is like a swinging hammock, to be played with as cats claw at a ball of yarn. Whatever way you interpret the events of yesteryear, the history of the region has been carved, etched, and blasted into its architecture, economy, and the DNA of its inhabitants. It can be seen in street names and park plaques, in family stories and living memory, as well as in what is taught (or not) to our children. While the national history books may skirt around our less palatable past, it has resolutely made Britain who we are today, and the North is no exception.

I used to think that history was boring, but mostly because I didn't understand its relevance to my life at that time. Now I understand that history is not something separate from us, boxed off neatly elsewhere, but that it is knotted to us, even if that string seems invisible unless you know how and where to look. Just read any story depicting time travel, warning that altering anything in the past can have huge consequences for the future. Likewise, what we do in the present can greatly affect what's to come, so here's to choosing the next steps for our region wisely.

III. Class and the Classroom

Northerners today might relate to the 1967 comedy sketch 'The Four Yorkshiremen'. In it, four men in white suits sit drinking fine wine (said blokes are John Cleese, Graham Chapman, Marty Feldman, and Tim Brooke-Taylor). As they marvel over their current lifestyle, they begin to muse how forty years ago they'd have been glad of a cup of cold tea to round of assenting 'ayes': one says they drank out of a rolled-up newspaper for lack of cups; another that they had to suck on a piece of damp cloth. What follows is progressively absurd quibbling over who had the most deprived upbringing. Despite their hardships, they end the sketch wondering if they were happier when they were poor and lament the ignorance of the youth of today. I literally cried laughing when I watched this for the first time because I have heard a similar trope many a-time from every member of my family born before the 1960s. My grandma would often mutter: "You don't know you were born, you..." when I would leave milk at the end of my bowl of cereal or attempt to convince my mum, once again, that I needed a horse. The latter was never successful, as she always replied with "I had to make do with riding cows on our smallholding", though they didn't buy me a cow to ride either. But our elders may have a point. My parents certainly didn't have the privileges my sister and I grew up with.

Neither of my parents went to university, my dad entering the fire service at sixteen, not a fan of academic pursuits; my mum unable to afford it. Mum was born in the bath at her grandma's house in Rossendale, growing up in the former textile town of Rawtenstall in a home that still had an outside toilet. She spent her teen years in a single-parent household, wearing clothes made by grandma so she could keep up with the latest fashions they couldn't afford. Mum worked weekends at the local market selling fruit and veg, and spent her spare time 'welly cobbing' in the field outside her local pub, which involved lobbing a wellington boot backwards over your head to see who could get it the farthest. Although she had a place at a local grammar school to do her A Levels, she ended up going to a secretarial college after her aunt and uncle, who had no children of their own, lent my grandma the money to send her there so she could start earning faster. After my sister and I were in school, she started teaching typewriting at a Further Education college. When colleges required formal qualifications for teachers in the mid-1990s, she gained a Cert. Ed and a Princess Di haircut along with it.

Despite this lack of initial access to higher education and the cultural capital it affords, my grandma played organ at church and taught my mum to play piano; reading featured heavily in their household; and the idea of good 'education' was strong centring around always saying your 'Ps and Qs', wearing your Sunday Best to church, and observing strict table manners. Much to my mum's frustration, I was "unteachable" when it came to the piano, wanting to add my own notes in rather than read the music (I argue I could have been a jazz musician if my creativity hadn't been stifled). Much to my dad's frustration, they didn't manage to pass the table manners to me either, as I apparently ate "like an American".

Actual American Bill Bryson (eating habits unknown) observed on the bus from Manchester to Wigan "how neat and well looked after were the endless terraces of little houses... Everything about them bespoke an air of modesty and make-do, but every stoop shone, every window gleamed, every sill had a fresh, glossy coat of paint." This could be said for many parts of the North. The front cover of the book *It's an Old Lancashire Custom* has a black and white photo of a well-built woman of advanced age on her knees in her pinny, scrubbing the pavement outside what is presumably her house with a bucket of soap suds. The image reminds me of my maternal grandma, though she'd not appreciate that, preferring to be remembered looking smart with her perm done properly. My mum tells me that my grandma used to finish off their newly mopped front steps with a 'donkey stone' that you could buy from the rag-and-bone man to give the edges a finish. This technique started in the mill towns of the North to clean greasy mill stairways, later becoming popular with housewives when, according to Sylvia Corbridge "a donkey-stoned front doorstep, a crisp cotton lace curtain and a pot plant in the window were symbols of modest prosperity and impeccable housewifery." Women could even be seen hanging out of their window frames, legs dangling inside, scrubbing the outside glass. This approach to housekeeping lost popularity in the 1960s, as I assume women were too busy burning their bras, or other things second-wave feminists were doing back then, to bother scrubbing a step. Saying that, even today as my parents live their newly found middle-class lifestyle, my mum still cleans the windows with vinegar – something her aunt did with newspaper all her life, "and she always had shiny winders" – and my dad did the outsides until he hit seventy and we insisted he stopped climbing ladders as it was giving us all anxiety.

Southern Comedienne Angela Barnes jokes about how to tell if someone is working-class, explaining that if you compliment them on something they're wearing, they will instantly tell you where they got it from and how much it cost: "Tenner, Tesco." The joke rings true as I usually respond with either, "it was me mum's" (we swap clothes a lot) or "charity shop, fiver!" Just this week I told a friend I liked her jeans and she replied: "Six quid from New Look."

Alternatively, Rochdale writer Mark Hodkinson offers the quicker approach of simply seeing how someone pronounces the word "class". Despite my own pronunciation – 'class' rhymes with 'ass' not 'arse' – I'm arguably the most culturally middle-class person in my family as a vegetarian, *Guardian* reading, world travelling doctor (though not the useful, life-saving kind). I say 'culturally' because financially I still have to watch those pennies, as teaching jobs in the third sector don't exactly rake in the brass, though I was raised to live 'within my means'. But it's all relative. While my great auntie used to complain that she couldn't understand me as I sounded too "posh", one of the first things my Southern housemates at uni did was tease me for sounding common when I pronounced 'cup' with a Northern vowel sound.

My dad's grandad worked in a rope factory in Preston. When his wife ran off and left him with four kids to look after, he opened a General Store in the village of Longton. My mum's grandma, a housewife, moved from Burnley to Rossendale when my great grandad took a job as an overseer at Folly Mill. She made the local paper when she turned ninety, as she had an 'open house' to celebrate, and a journalist came to immortalise the moment. When asked her secret to long life she said: "I have a good family and have been well looked after. It could be the Rossendale air, too – although it is a lot colder up here in Crawshawbooth. My husband used to say it was like Siberia sometimes!" The males of my grandparents' generation were recruited into the armed forces and, luckily for all involved, survived the Second World War whereafter one became a car mechanic, the other a firefighter. My grandmas were, respectively, a cleaner and a cook, and their brothers and sisters all worked in the shoe, rope, and weaving factories of the region. One grandma then got remarried to a firefighter she met while cooking at the firehouse, later becoming a hairdresser and setting up her own salon. My grandad sometimes joined her there, washing ladies' hair and chatting to them, providing some eye candy for the loyal blue rinse customers, as he had an old movie star look about him (if that movie star was aged and rotund and wore hand-knitted vest tops). The marriage resolutely more successful than the last, they moved to the Lancastrian-Cumbrian border in their retirement, quietly and happily getting old and fat together on homemade scones and trifles.

My parents' generation ended up in different jobs, though a common thread is that my family supplied a steady stream of staff to Lancashire's fire stations (maternal grandad, grandma, great uncle, uncle, mum, and dad). My dad joined the fire service aged sixteen and my mum met him when she moved from answering emergency phone calls to being his secretary. The only time I ever remember being hit by my dad was when he caught me playing with matches as a child. My later love for burning incense and candles as a teen also caused much anxiety and grumbling (though no further corporal punishment). An uncle was also briefly a firefighter who married a travel agent; the other became a driving instructor and married a nurse; and my auntie a shop assistant who married a lorry driver. One family member originally followed in his father's footsteps by joining the army, but promptly ran away when he was handed his soldier underwear with "Her Majesty's Prison" stamped on them.

Fast-forward to my generation, and jobs have again changed, with industry moving towards service economy work in bars, restaurants, and call centres. I've been working since I was twelve in a range of part-time jobs from kennel worker to sandwich maker, dish washer and Avon Lady, customer service phone answerer, pub bartender, and Spar cashier (a perk of which was getting to take home 10p pasties at the end of the day). From a young age, my parents taught us to save our five and twenty pence pieces to put in the bank until, one day, my sister raided the at-home piggy bank, accidentally dropping the solid metal container on her foot, relieving her of her big toenail in the process. You reap what you sow.

Even where jobs remain the same, writer Tim Worstall argued in *The Guardian* that a plumber or cabby might eat their tea at 6pm then go off to play darts and drink beer, but being a home owner with an income of up to £100k, which he might spend on foreign holidays, he's "bourgeois with some working-class habits." Though the cost-of-living crisis might change our social landscape yet again, there's something worth delving into about the changing nature of class with its complex cultural, social, and economic facets.

I'm what they call a first-generation university attendee. Thanks in part to student loans, my older sister led the way, attending Durham University (though she found herself not living in the quaint centre but just outside of Middlesbrough which, at the time, was infamous for having a large number of people addicted to crack). I followed in our mother's footsteps by becoming an educator, my sister an editor. Today, we straddle two worlds with one foot in working-class stories and values, thriftiness, personal humility and regional pride, and the other in the middle-class world with our degrees, love of (and ability to) travel, and appreciation for a continental cheese board with olives. She ended up with a MSc, and I now have a PhD.

According to the Council of Graduate Schools, only about three percent of first-generation uni-goers pursue doctoral studies. The leap from no degree to a doctorate was quite a big one for our family. This meant that they had no idea what I was doing for many years. When I'd inform my dad of my latest publication, he'd predictably respond asking me if I got paid for it. I'd remind him what I'd told him before: that you don't get paid for academic articles. "What's the point of doing it then?" He'd then make a disapproving noise and continue whatever he was doing before. Aside from the noble goal of sharing knowledge, universities want their employees to publish. Such articles then (in theory at least) help you secure a job. However, even my doctorate isn't enough to entirely erase the effects of class as, according to a 2024 *Financial Times* article, first-generation PhD-holders are less likely to get permanent academic positions, and more likely to be at lower-ranked institutions. Carolyn Kay Steedman wrote eloquently in her 1986 non-fiction, *Landscape for a Good Woman: A Story of Two Lives,* about navigating the borderlands between an academic world and her working-class upbringing with her Lancashire mother. She describes how, upon meeting a woman at a party in London, she has the powerful realisation that, a hundred years ago, she'd have been cleaning the woman's shoes. As pointed out by working-class academics Pat Mahony and Christine Zmroczek, class is less a past footprint and more a foot that carries us forward.

So where does this leave us? Can I confidently call myself middle-class? Does it even matter? A 2013 study by a collaboration of British sociologists found that the traditional class divides no longer hold in the twenty-first century, instead outlining seven new classes: the precariat (low social, economic, and cultural capital); emergent service workers (young urbanites with high social and cultural capital but low economic capital); the traditional working-class (who are often homeowners over sixty years of age); new affluent workers (landing middle scores across all types of capital); the technical middle class (prosperous but culturally apathetic and socially isolated); the established middle-class (scoring high economically, socially, and culturally); and the elite. The largest group were the established middle-class at 20 per cent and the smallest groups were the elite and technical middle-class, both at six per cent.

I did the survey and came out as an emergent service worker: high cultural but low economic capital. This makes sense to me as degrees can teach you a lot, but not necessarily the 'hidden curriculum' of academic or industry, nor can they promise you the connections you need to get into well-paying jobs. A more pedestrian example of this uneven capital is that, while at university, I made the decision not to shop on the high street anymore as I didn't want to be part of the supply chain that resulted in masses of waste produced by fast fashion and the exploitative/slave labour used to make it. There was one problem: I couldn't afford the expensive Fair-Trade stores that seemed to be aimed at middle-aged, middle-class women. My solution was the humble charity shop where one person's trash is another person's treasure. Guilt-free rummaging is hands-down a favourite activity of mine, a pastime hailing back to childhood. My maternal grandma – a working-class mother who lived through the rationing of the Second World War – knew how to shop cheap. I grew up going to car boot sales and charity shops with her in search of a good bargain. In the area of Lancashire where she lived, many of the high streets were whittled down to mostly charity shops anyway, with a spattering of independent stores with names like 'Sunday Best' or corner shops, the rest boarded-up buildings awaiting a new lease of life. Back in Chester, a place known for high street and designer shopping, as a teenager, I'd look both ways before entering a charity shop in case someone from school saw me and yelled "scav" at me. As an adult, I no longer worry about this as, aside from no longer carrying teen anxiety about what other people think of my shopping choices, at some point along the way second-hand became trendy.

Scouser Jen Graham, aka Charity Shop Girl, has contributed to recent revitalisation of the 'second-hand revolution' in the UK since posting her finds on social media after getting laid off during the pandemic. Incidentally, a Facebook group that got me through the early days of the lockdown was called 'Terrible Art in Charity Shops.' People from all over the world sharing a love for naff donated creations, which turned into recreating said art from home as people couldn't get out there to find new pieces. Comedy gold – and a surprising amount of people willing to get naked in the name of entertainment.

My sister and I are not the only ones in our generation who benefitted from the social mobility of the '90s. The North, used to being the poor cousin of the South and denied the rewards of the taxpayers' pounds, received investment (and a lot of EU money) in the '80s and '90s. The results have been patchy but cities like Liverpool, Manchester, and Leeds have thrived (Manchester has even been described as the UK's Barcelona, though I think that's a tad generous). In the nineteenth century, Liverpool was known as the city of gentlemen, rich from white-collar trading, and Manchester the city of men working blue-collar factory jobs without help from the monarchy or aristocracy. However, '70s Liverpool, according to Stuart Maconie, became a caricature of "'taches, perms, robbery and signing on" and I'd argue that, in the '90s,

Liverpool still seemed to be associated with getting robbed or battered on a night out.

In turn, '90s Manchester was described, somewhat dismissively, by Bill Bryson as "an airport with a city attached" despite being the up-and-coming economic powerhouse (albeit with its share of gang problems, garnering it the unfortunate nickname of 'Gunchester'). But fast-forward to the twenty-first century and things have changed. In the BBC Three sketch by Brennan Reece, a baritone (Southern) voice describes industrialisation and poverty, calling the North "nature's dustbin", emerges from peeing behind a tree to argue "mate, have you even been the North? Like, we've done it up... Cobble stones and hung up washing lines, that's all gone now. I've got a washing machine. I've got two bloody fridges!" A pause. "Although one of them is unplugged and it's out in the yard." Nothing's perfect. Manchester remains the powerhouse of the North and one of the fastest growing cities in Europe. A noughties edition of *Lonely Planet* argued that Manchester was "looking up. Gone are the Dickensian days of grinding poverty. Gone too the gloom 'n' doom of the 1980s indie punk scene and its Joy Division pessimism: over the last 15 years the city has developed a champagne-for-breakfast insouciance and an almost giddy attitude towards fun." Though I'd argue there was nothing wrong with the moody music scene, and that champers for breakfast is a questionable measure of success. Not to be outdone, Liverpool won the accolade of European City of Culture in 2008. Upon hearing this, I'll admit that I was initially a bit baffled, but have since fallen in love with the place: the docks, the architecture, the accents, and – if you're into theology or architecture – not one but two cathedrals. One is Catholic and locally known as 'Paddy's Wigwam' due to its conical design and the other is Anglican and wins the title of biggest cathedral in England. You can also find the so-called 'bombed out church', destroyed during the Liverpool Blitz of 1941 which reduced 70 per cent of houses in the area to rubble. While they were rebuilt, the skeleton of the church remains, an icon of the city.

That said, the trend of investing in progress was somewhat reversed in the aftermath of the economic crisis of 2008. Since 2010, the government's much-discussed austerity measures have eroded people's safety nets, and it shows. I remember visiting Manchester about five years ago and being shocked at the levels of homelessness. When I used to go as a kid, there were perhaps a couple of rough sleepers. Now you have to step over scores of legs circling paper coffee cups with a few coins in them to get anywhere downtown. Figures show the number of people sleeping on the streets went from below ten at one point to the hundreds in the mid-2010s. When lockdown began in early 2020, the government showed what was possible, scooping everyone into temporary accommodation. People had access not only to a safe space but also mental health services, addiction counselling, and help navigating the benefits system. This support ended later that year when we churned people back out onto the rainy streets of Manchester. Despite this, Andy Burnham reported at the end of 2021 that numbers of rough sleepers in Greater Manchester were down from 268 in 2017 to 89.

Halfway through 2020 I moved to Manchester and, for those not comprising the precariat, it's not a bad decision. According to a 2020 article in *Conde Nast Traveller*, five of the six coolest neighbourhoods in the UK are in the North, listing Ancoats, Manchester; Whitley Bay, Newcastle; Aigburth, Liverpool; Mabgate, Leeds; and Sharrow Vale, Sheffield as post-industrial cities "busy fostering an indie attitude". I appreciate the sentiment, though it makes the cities sound like hipsters who wear glasses they don't need. The sixth place listed in the article is Stirchley in Birmingham, so the South didn't even get a look in. I nearly studied at

Newcastle and loved how you could step off the campus and straight onto the high street (Charles Jennings argues that Newcastle is like Lisbon in that they're both a bit cut off from the rest of civilisation, are slightly mad, and like to eat and drink a lot). I ended up choosing Leeds, however, so I can vouch for it being a great (the youth in Leeds today would probably say "sick") place to live. Since the '90s, Simon Armitage argued that the city put its "new dosh" into its "tarted-up streets and tarted-up shops." Some might argue that, in tarting these areas up, they have lost their beloved grit, but I'll leave you with Stuart Maconie's argument: "Some local naysayers have already begun to describe the Calls area as 'yuppified', which is intended as an insult but I prefer it to 'run-down shithole.'" The same could be said of Whitley Bay, a town my mate has just moved to. She is loving the cute cafes and weekly dolphin and seal sightings (though when I went to visit, the sea fret was so thick we couldn't see the sand, let alone frolicking sea life). Though I guess one person's rejuvenation is another person's gentrification.

My hometown won the accolade of the second-best place to live in the Northwest in the *Sunday Times* Best Places to Live 2020 list (after Altringham in Greater Manchester) and the 2021 most beautiful city in the whole of the UK list, using an Ancient Greek mathematical 'Golden Ratio' to assess the buildings. Liverpool's Port ranked pretty high too. When I was looking at places in Manchester, one well-meaning landlady responded, incredulously, "Chester's lovely. Are you sure you'd rather live in Manchester?!" Not exactly the best sales pitch. York won first place of 2020 *The Times* list, which I'd say is deserved with its rambling streets and leaning Shambles.

Despite the face of the North having altered in many places, some stereotypes cling on, particularly in areas that have not changed much over the years. I found a *Guardian* article entitled 'Let's move to Lancaster, Lancashire: it's grander than you might think', which has as its encouragement a kind of back-handed compliment or reference to people's disbelief that it might actually be an alright place to reside. Across the north, long forgotten are the slagheaps and slums and smoke-filled air of yesteryear and former mills are now either gone, derelict with TO LET signs, or converted into trendy office spaces or apartments.

In an attempt to decentralise the historical concentration of all-that-is-good from London, the BBC signalled its move up North in 2004, and a number of other TV channels followed suit, leading to the current two-hundred-acre MediaCityUK site emerging in Salford. Screen Yorkshire is also a strong regional media production company responsible for a number of productions, and Channel Four opened an office in Leeds in 2020 to change "what has been practically a creative wasteland for television outside of London for decades." In 2016, politician George Osbourne talked of encouraging a 'northern powerhouse', investing £60 million in transport links east to west and reducing travel times to and from the capital. He also announced an additional £20m a year to close the educational achievement gaps but, before you get too excited, all of this is against an austerity backdrop that saw £3.6 billion removed from the North via public spending cuts, while the South saw a £4.7 billion rise. There were even whispers of moving a parliamentary base to Manchester and/or York. Such changes would be great news for the many Northerners who feel they must migrate south to pursue their dream career, though with Brexit and Covid taking the main stage, the idea of Northern investment seems to have slipped off the political agenda for now.

Returning to the cultural heritage of the region, London might have the Big Ben and the Tate, but Chester has the second most photographed clock in England and Liverpool has the Tate Modern. The last time I was at the Tate Modern

Once, I participated in a collaborative poem creation; a nice memory which made up for the first time I went to the gallery and left disgruntled by parrots in bare cages for no apparent reason and a video of sex workers bribed with smack to allow the 'artist' to tattoo them; two ethically questionable exhibits. Another vivid modern art experience 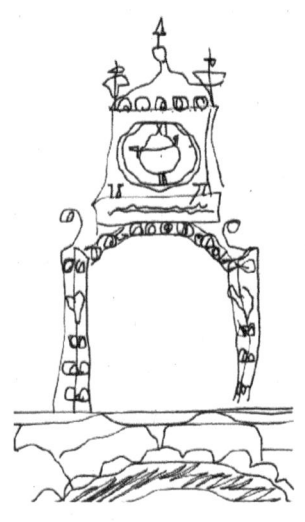 was in Leeds. I went to an exhibition with an Oxbridge-educated anaesthetist, and we fell out about it afterwards. We walked into an empty white room with what looked like a giant condom hanging from the ceiling and there was an upturned polystyrene box with a ball of foil on top. It looked like they hadn't cleared the room out yet and I nearly asked the attendant where the art was. That was the art, apparently. I was extremely dubious whilst my date blabbed on about it being something visionary, though I'm 90 per cent sure he was winding me up (conceptual minimalist art just isn't for me).

Likewise, Gloucester might have a cheese rolling competition, but Cumbria has a gurning contest in which the victor warps their face into the most absurd contortion. Sometimes with their head in a toilet seat. But what was I saying? Oh aye, that we're cultured up North. Salford has the Lowry Museum – an homage to the great painter of the Northern industrial scene and matchstick people. L.S. Lowry used to paint landscapes, saying he didn't see the beauty of Manchester at first, "then one day I saw it... I saw the beauty of the streets and the crowds." Lowry lived with his elderly mother his whole life until he retired to Cheshire (a part that is now Greater Manchester), apparently adorning his room with numerous clocks all telling different times because he didn't want to know the real time. I don't know why he didn't just get rid of the lot, but then maybe I don't understand creative genius. I grew up with one of Lowry's scenes in our front room which went to my grandma's when my parents moved and, when she died, went to the charity shop. My mum and I argue over which painting it was because, despite seeing it daily for eighteen years, his urban depictions look pretty similar to the casual observer. Whichever it was, I hope it found a good home.

My county is also home to Jodrell Bank, a radio observatory that is a UNESCO World Heritage Site due to its contributions towards understanding our universe, a location frequented by many a-gaggle of school children who visit to learn about all the mysterious stuff floating in outer space. Simon Armitage poetically (and maybe generously) described its dish as a big yacht sailing proudly across Cheshire. Another Cheshire favourite for school trips was the Catalyst Museum, a mind-boggling place for primary school children filled with interactive science experiments which translates as stuff to poke your hands in. Adult me returned with my friend and her two young girls hoping to recreate the magic I had remembered, though it seemed they hadn't updated anything since I'd last been and the carpet looked like it needed a good scrub.

When it comes to museums, I'll admit that the South does have the incredible Natural History Museum in Oxford with its café viewing gallery that overlooks a giant T-Rex skeleton. The downstairs Pitt Rivers exhibitions from around the world are also fascinating, though we should probably give back all the royal jewellery and shrunken heads we nicked. Comedian

James Acaster, in his skit about London's British Museum, argues that "finders keepers, shut up" is probably not a long-term solution to the pillage of countries' sacred artefacts. Historically, even when we had valuable pieces up North, we were scorned. In 1857, a Manchester Art Treasures exhibition famously earned the following retort from the Duke of Devonshire: "What in the world do you want with art in Manchester? Why can't you stick to your cotton spinning." Elizabeth Gaskill's novel, *North and South*, touches on this stereotype, too: "The people here don't want to learn. They don't want books and culture. It's all money and smoke. That's what they eat and breathe." But Manchester folks argued that culture should be democratised, not a pleasure reserved for the elite. Two hundred years later, certain people are still not convinced, as an art critic was complaining on BBC Radio 4 that he hadn't seen some Caravaggios due to them being "hidden away" in places like Hull or Preston. *Guardian* editor Helen Pidd retorted that he spoke as if they'd been displayed on the moon, despite being sure he'd make the journey if they were somewhere like Paris. Even a Filey scientist on *Great British Railway Journeys* talking about a four-thousand-year-old skeleton suggested not many people knew about him because he was "tucked away in the North of England" – and she was from the North.

This idea of the South being the only place for anything half decent can be seen not only in bickering over art but also in art itself. Nineties television drama *Our Friends in the North* includes a scene where ambitious Geordie, Nicky, is told by his well-spoken Southern girlfriend that, if he wants to make a difference, he can't do it from Newcastle. Jokingly, in an episode of Yorkshire sitcom *Last of the Summer Wine*, Cleggy tells the others that the local librarian deserved sympathy because he had "intellectual aspirations" which meant that one day he would "lose all sense of reason and move down south." (I suppose my aspirations did move me south, if by south we mean south of the equator.) This predicament leaves us with a dual challenge of counteracting this stereotype of the North as uneducated whilst stopping the brain drain of its 'aspirational' people.

Diving back into history for a moment, if Northern children a hundred years ago didn't value school, perhaps it was because they knew that as soon as they finished, aged thirteen, they'd be off to work in t' mills or mines to make much needed money for their family. That said, not all learning comes from inside the four walls of a school. US writer Maya Angelou in *I Know Why the Caged Bird Sings* wrote about her neighbour teaching her that some folks who were unable to go to school were more educated or intelligent than university professors, and advised her to listen to what country people called "mother wit" as in those "homely sayings" was the collective wisdom of generations. This sentiment is echoed in advice from the 1950s, encouraging people to travel to Lancashire and "hear for yourself the speech of the older men and women...whose schooling was scanty but whose education has been rich."

But if you want to consider education in the sense of formal schooling, the North has many great universities such as the University of Leeds, which was good enough to attract the Southerners who taught me about the North-South divide in the first place, or the University of Manchester, where Ernest Rutherford split the atom in 1917, making scientific history. One of the earliest records of the relationship between the moon and the tides was written by Northumbrian Saint Bede in his eighth century book, *The Reckoning of Time*: "More marvellous than anything else is the great fellowship that exists between the ocean and the courses of the moon. For at the moon's every rising and sitting, the ocean sends forth the strength of its ardour, and when it retreats, it lays them bare. It's as if the ocean were dragged forward against its will by certain exhalations of the moon and when her path ceases, it's poured back again into its proper measure."

As well as those accolades, the oldest public library in the English-speaking world is Chetham's Library in Manchester which opened in 1653 and has been in continuous use ever since. Then, in 1852 Charles Dickens formally opened the first free lending library a 'special provision for the working classes', which is now Manchester Central Library. Which brings us to the issue of education and accessibility: when people have access to quality education, they can flourish.

Trips to our local library were the highlight of my week as my sister and I devoured books at a pace that meant we couldn't have bought one every time we wanted to read. Public libraries expand opportunities for learning to everyone, not only to those who can afford private collections. I remember taking a group of refugee children to the local library for the first time, accompanied by a father getting his head around the concept: "So you can take a book? You don't have to pay? You just bring it back when you're finished? We don't have anything like this in our country. This is good." I suppose in a capitalist world, it is quite a novel concept.

Seaside towns that have seen better days like Blackpool and Scarborough often suffer from brain drain as young people who leave to get a degree often don't come back, whilst, to the south, Brighton and Bournemouth have their own campuses. Austerity further hit such towns as public sector cuts led to jobs lost and council budgets tightened. In 2017, government investment figures showed Yorkshire and the Humber with £8,791 a year spending per head compared to London at £10,129, with the Northwest at £9,387 and the Northeast at £9,472 per head. Whilst London got some £50 million for a fancy garden bridge, the Institute for Public Policy Research revealed this was more than the whole of the

North received during the same period. They got expensive garden decorations and we got the middle finger.

So, if you're still thinking Northerners are uncultured or uneducated, let me shift the framing slightly: the government has invested in culture and education in the South meaning that more cultural activities can bloom, and students can flourish. It's not surprising, then, if the opposite is true for areas without this kind of input and support. As argued in a 2020 *Economist* article, Britain is the most regionally unequal rich country in that, whilst other countries have poor bits, Britain has a poor half.

In my own educational experience, in contrast with my sweet little village primary school, my high school was the largest comprehensive in the city where it was best to pretend you didn't like learning and be scary enough that no-one would start a fight with you. I wouldn't say a pervasive anti-school attitude is unusual in the North as, in writer Mark Hodkinson's 2022 *No One Round Here Reads Tolstoy: Memoirs of a Working-Class Reader*, he similarly laments that at his school in Rochdale he had to hide his intelligence and learn how to survive among hostility. When I got my A Level results, a friend of a friend said to me, accusingly: "I didn't know you were clever." I did not, as you might imagine, take this as an insult. Instead, I was pretty pleased with myself as she'd only ever seen me mucking about in class, as I did the work quickly then messed about with friends who didn't want to do the work at all. The aim of the game for our long-suffering Headmistress seemed to be keeping the riff raff in line and dragging the failing students up to a C grade: those of us who earned As were left to our own devices.

In contrast with private schools that had debate teams and chess clubs and university prep classes, there were few after-school activities aside from music and annual school plays. I did both, and on my first week of choir got yelled at by the deputy headmaster for singing too loudly on our way out of the building. My career guidance included a multiple-choice questionnaire which told me I should be a gardener based solely on the fact I said I liked plants, though I ended up doing my work placement at a hairdresser's where I swept the floor and made coffees for a week. One teacher asked if I was going to apply for Oxbridge. "I don't know. Should I?" was my reply. His sole advice was to read the *Economist*, and this interaction culminated in an extremely embarrassing interview at Cambridge where I was hideously underprepared when asked to give my opinion on the war in Iraq. I think I mumbled a response along the lines of "something about oil". My parents, who'd driven me down and bought me new shoes for the occasion, and I passed one of the interviewers on the street afterwards and he tried (and failed) to hide a smirk. The memory of the day still makes me cringe.

The historical North-South divide in terms of both wealth and education continues today in terms of (private) schooling, grades, and whether children are more likely or not to attend university in the first place, with London and the Southeast way ahead of the North. Part of this is a vicious cycle as poorer children are more likely to go to worse schools as ranked by Ofsted ratings, so you don't need a university degree to understand the link between regional poverty and educational attainment. The Northeast has a particularly high percentage of children on free school meals and any educator can tell you that children will struggle to concentrate on maths when they are hungry. During the pandemic, twenty-two-year-old Manchester United footballer, Marcus Rashford, ended up publicly shaming PM Boris Johnson into not closing the school meals scheme over the summer holidays for the most vulnerable kids.

If you follow British news, you may have heard that, since

2013, white working-class boys became the latest educational worry, replacing black boys in the so-called "race to the bottom". While the performance of some minority pupils has improved over the past two decades, that of white working-class boys has apparently stagnated and they are the least likely to go to university. Those boys from the Northwest, it is claimed, have less social mobility than children of colour in London. This discrepancy could be down to the fact that for every pound invested in London, the government knows it can make two pounds back. Allocate that same amount in the North, and you might only see fifty pence. This makes for a cycle of underinvestment and underdevelopment. Sceptics, however, argue that this sudden concern for white working-class boys was the Right's response to the Black Lives Matter movement. There's much to unpack in terms of race, class, and regional deprivation. As easy as it is to claim clear boundaries by race or region, it is not as simple as South = rich, North = poor, as there are concentrations of poverty in the major cities of London and Birmingham and pockets of middle-class places in the North like Harrogate or Cheshire's rich towns and villages. London hip hop educator, Akala, writes about the intersections of race and class with poverty and substandard education in his 2019 book, *Natives*, and writer Reni Eddo-Lodge argues that instead of a white man in a flat cap, the working-class today is "a black woman pushing a pram". Though, going off the 2013 categories, maybe a more accurate category would be 'the precariat'. Author of *Chavs: The Demonisation of the Working Class*, Owen Jones, argues for the modern symbol of the working-class to be a part-time female shelf-stacker. So, the issue isn't straightforward, though perhaps we can agree that where money goes, so goes decent education and opportunities for work.

The EU referendum of 2016 showed us that a North-South

divide still firmly exists. Whilst the North of England used to be a red shirt tucked into the South's blue trousers, this voting pattern has shifted over time. The majority in Manchester, Liverpool, and Newcastle voted Remain while the rest of the North voted Leave. Many liberals scorned folks who voted the latter, and back came the stereotype of the uneducated North. Many Americans claimed they voted for Donald Trump because they were sick of politicians – and liberals dismissing them as idiots didn't undo his victory. In a similar vein, many voters here said they supported Brexit to get rid of one more layer of faraway bureaucrats telling them what to do and giving away their industry; a way to give the finger to Westminster. This may well by the case, though this narrative ignores the fact that migrants were – and still are – made a convenient scapegoat around larger economic issues at home and abroad and became the subsequent collateral damage. So when political alternatives included bumbling Boris and fibbing Farage as the leaders on offer, we need to listen to the whys of voters' dissatisfaction as well as the hows of the latter's successful campaigns in positioning themselves as representing "the people" without being honest about which people they really mean, or what kind of people they really are. It was said that many Leave voters came from low-income former manufacturing areas with high unemployment which could give us a clue to such discontent. With that said, national politicians getting their heads out of Westminster and into the streets seems like a good place to start, supporting local representatives to invest in areas left forgotten. As well as employment this should include better education – one that includes media literacy and the value of multiculturalism, as well as critical thinking and problem-solving for an inclusive twenty-first century (and by "inclusive" I'm talking about region and class and race and immigration – it doesn't have to be a zero-sum game).

The storyline plotting the North-South divide thickened as the pandemic trundled on and areas in the North seemed to be hardest hit by Covid-19 as the leaves turned brown in 2020. In October, the Northwest was the worst affected area with 643 cases per 100,000 in Liverpool and 605.5 cases in Burnley in comparison with 352 in Brighton and 34.71 in Dover, and London boroughs ranging from 52 and 141. At one point, Manchester and Liverpool were the worst affected cities in England with Manchester with an 'R' rate ten times higher than the national average in October. As the government created a tiered system of action and Liverpool was placed on the highest tier and thus had the toughest restrictions, Manchester decided to resist. Without a full lockdown, businesses were not eligible for government support and, as argued by Labour's Manchester Mayor Andy Burnham, the North was already economically deprived in many areas so further restrictions would ruin the economy, which is also a factor in any region's public health. Burnham stood at the site of the Peterloo massacre almost two hundred years later and invoked the spirits of the past protesters to question the government's handling of the crisis, claiming regional bias. One Prestonian Twitter user, Dave Thorp (The Strictly Spoiler) observed:

Looking like we could be heading to an episode of Game of Thrones ... *Waiting for Andy Burnham to be declared King In The North and call his bannermen to march on the blond haired pretender ruling in the south ... The free folk north of the wall (aka Scotland) are welcome to join us.*

Winter was indeed coming, and the government had the unenviable job of balancing mental and physical health along the wobbling tightrope of Covid and economic deprivation as the so-called 'Northern Revolt' rumbled on. Hopping on the band wagon of mayors getting shit done, London mayor Sadiq Khan was re-elected in 2021 and pledged to bridge the North-South divide, visiting a number of places and schmoozing with the locals. Despite such pledges, sadly but perhaps not surprisingly, things have not yet bounced back post-pandemic in the already deprived areas of the North. In 2023, Knowsley in Merseyside was the second poorest town in England and a community space with a "social supermarket" run by a former Labour councillor served around 150 in 2020, just over 700 in 2021, and by the end of 2022 1,193 people.

Another facet of a Northern Revolt can be seen in the Northern Independence Party, founded in 2020. Northumberland writer Alex Niven described it as "a project that is mindful of the risks of cliché and nostalgia when it comes to defining the northern cause. Instead of pious avowals of northern identity, NIP's social media pages reclaim and refract stereotypes about northern culture with stylised portraits of whippets and tongue-in-cheek calls to nationalise Greggs and ban Dominic Cummings from Barnard Castle." One of the latest NIP mottos states: "We joke but we're serious", which I think sums up Northerners pretty well.

Newcastle lecturer Niven further argued that, over the past few years, the North has become "a blank slate for whichever stereotypes the London-based media wants to foist on it." The NIP is pushing back on this and what it may lack in electoral clout, it makes up for in playful cultural reclamation and calls for economic redistribution on behalf of a region that's fed up with being written off. When male life expectancy differs from 83.9 years in Westminster compared with 74.5 years in Blackpool, we know we have a problem. Although the North-South divide may not be what it used to be, it still exists and is a social justice issue that we could do with addressing.

IV. God's Own Country

I've had the privilege of visiting many areas of natural beauty around the world and, on the days when rain isn't lashing you in the face, the British Isles is no exception. Yorkshire folk claim their county, England's largest, as 'God's own country'. My mum reckons that's Lancashire, but she's outnumbered on that one, I think. Either way, God's country is firmly in the North. The South has the Cotswolds, the Southern coast, and the Downs, but the North has the country's backbone, the Pennine Way, the Yorkshire moors, the Lancashire forests, Hadrian's Wall, the beaches and cliffs of the Northeast coast, and the Lakes.

English writer and lover of the North, John Ruskin, is reported to have said, wisely, that: "Nature is painting for us, day after day, pictures of infinite beauty, if only we have the eyes to see them." No matter the progress or palaver occurring in our cities, the landscape of the North remains resolute, once a refuge from factory smog, now from road traffic and office life. The hills and lakes look on, sculpted by erosion here and there, but a steady constant, quietly tolerating our comings and goings.

If you're not from the North, perhaps you've not explored our neck of the woods much. Bryson declared he found "Southerners and Northerners were so extraordinarily, sometimes defiantly, ignorant of the geography of the other end of their country", with Southerners not being able to distinguish between the Yorkshires, and Northerners looking nervous when he said he used to live in Surrey "as if they were afraid I was going to say, 'Now you show me on the map just where that is.'" As such, this chapter is both an ode to the Northern countryside, as well as an education for any non-Northern readers who can empathise with Bill's observation.

Bryson also complained that being in the UK is like living in a Tupperware box as there's always a lid of clouds over the land. Yet come pelting rain or sporadic shine, walkers will walk and ramblers will ramble across the Isles. Whether farmers like it or not (and I suspect some don't, based on signage I've seen), British farmland is criss-crossed with pathways along hedgerows, across hillsides, through forests and cornfields. And for such access to public footpaths, we should probably thank the Kinder Scout Mass Trespassers. In 1932, hundreds of ramblers and members of the Young Communist League headed over to the Derbyshire Peak District to protest the lack of access to open areas of countryside in England and Wales after a group of walkers had been expelled from the area weeks earlier. The mobile protest was organised largely by Benny Rothman, a Romanian Jew from Manchester, and some argue that the trespass led to the 1949 National Parks legislation which protected walkers' rights and helped pave the establishment of the Pennine Way that so many of us know and love.

This love that can be felt when walking in nature is something worth fighting for. A French group called the Lettrists came up with the term 'psychogeography' in the mid-1950s to describe how places carry not only history but human emotion within them. They concocted this idea after (inebriated) wandering around Paris with the belief that aimless 'drifting' was the best way to tap into the soul of a city; to feel how humans have shaped place and space and vice versa, linking earth, mind, and body. The idea can also apply to the fields and footpaths carved out over rural areas. Though it might have taken some male intellectuals to name it, this was something women had already talked about, in particular Yorkshirewoman, Emily Brontë, who had written about this kind of unplanned meandering in a nineteenth century poem:

I'll walk where my own nature would be leading:
It vexes me to choose another guide:
Where the gray flocks in ferny glens are feeding;
Where the wild wind blows on the mountain side.

What have those lonely mountains worth revealing?
More glory and more grief than I can tell:
The earth that wakes one human heart to feeling
Can centre both the worlds of Heaven and Hell.

Not everyone is a fan of a ramble, though. Doncaster-born TV personality Jeremy Clarkson wrote that walking was pointless when you just pass a bunch of trees then end up back where you started. He then, however, bought a farm in Oxfordshire and finally went for a walk around it at the grand age of sixty and discovered the joys of rambling around the countryside. (Or at least his countryside. He tried – and failed – to remove the public footpath rights from his land on the Isle of Man). Like Clarkson, Covid-19 also tried to limit public footpath access. The idyllic pastime was scuppered by the pandemic when people were initially banned from travelling to exercise after hundreds flocked to roomy areas of natural beauty, with one *Daily Mash* journalist expounding: "Wander lonely as a cloud like Wordsworth, until someone shatters your peace with a potential Covid-sneeze and you run home to Ozark." (To avoid meeting others, Simon Armitage helpfully suggested Northumberland for those wanting either rural seclusion, or a place to go barmy without anyone knowing or caring.)

Walking for me is a family tradition – over t' Lancashire crags, in the Lake District, into the nearby Welsh hills and mountains. In retirement, my maternal grandparents hauled their trusty caravan all over the UK, stopping to have their sarnies with a flask of tea overlooking some vista – often from the safety of the Volvo if it was too rainy or windy. After her husband died, my grandma moved back to Rossendale, adopted a sweet little dog, and I would sometimes join them on their hillside walks. Poppy was a Jack Russel-Pomeranian cross and loved diving down rabbit holes. Once we lost her for an entire day down one and it all got a bit *Watership Down* as we tried to coax and cajole, then flush her out. Later, when my parents retired, they joined a University of the Third Age walking group and, let me tell you, the oldies can walk for hours across fields, along canals, through forests and up hills, the latter dictated by the state of the current group's knees (though, luckily for them, Cheshire is pretty flat). Mark Hodkinson argued that "at times of turmoil or confusion, Rochdale people often 'take to the moors'" and during the pandemic lockdown many of us did just that. I relished my daily walks and, once it was legal, ventured further afield to explore when other activities were still on the no-go list. On days where I was restricted to my local area, I spent time reminiscing on places I'd been already as well as plotting sites that I would visit when I could.

Whilst some places you visit and go 'ahh, this is nice', 'pretty', or even 'beautiful', other places you visit and feel something that is sometimes hard to put into words. Travel writer Jini Reddy calls this the 'magic' in the landscape. Such landscape has inspired poets, notably Cumbrian William Wordsworth, who now has a whole area in the Lakes named 'Wordsworth Country' in his honour. Artists came from far and wide to appreciate the beauty of the area, such as John Constable, whose depiction of the Lake District I ate off for years, as they adorned my grandma's placemats. Not so much magical as decorative, but you can't expect to feel moved every time you have a bowl of cornflakes.

The Lake District is also home to the largest lake in England, Lake Windermere, ten and a half miles long and one mile wide. Obviously, this can't compete with Scotland, which has lochs big enough to hide Nessie in, but as far as England goes, it is unbeaten. Nineteenth century London art critic, instructor, and social reformer, John Ruskin, retired to and died in Cumbria, arguing "I do not know in all my country, still less in France or Italy, a place more naturally divine." His Brantwood house overlooking Coniston waters can be visited as an art centre and museum displaying Ruskin's furniture and belongings. I'll admit I've never actually been inside, but I did have a cracking cheese toasty from the adjoining café. My family and I often would stop at Ruskin's View as a kid – a vista overlooking the curving River Lune in Kirkby Lonsdale – after my grandma moved to the village of Over Kellet, near the Lancashire-Cumbria border. He reckoned the view was "one of the loveliest in England and therefore in the world" which is very patriotic but maybe a little overstated. Other smaller – but by no means lesser – lakes include my mum's favourite spot, Tarn Hows, which gets packed with people who apparently share this sentiment during high season when it's less likely to be lashing it down. I went midweek in the summer of 2022, and it was pretty peaceful and only mildly wet. Along the trail I added to the popular wish tree, pushing a two-pence piece into the rotten bark of a fallen trunk already peppered with the coins of past walkers. The Tarns came up for sale in 1929 and was bought by none other than Beatrix Potter, who later sold half to the National Trust and bequeathed them the other half upon her death. Writer Jennings didn't get what the fuss was about, describing it as filled with serious cagouled men and tiny grandmas walking their dogs up vertical fells. I'm not sure what fells he was looking at but it's not exactly Everest.

As well as the Lake District, we share a sizeable chunk of the Peak District, which spans five counties: Cheshire, Greater Manchester, and Yorkshire in the North; Derbyshire and Staffordshire in the Midlands. According to the National Trust, within the Peaks you can choose between visiting "grand houses, unspoiled moorland, rugged hillsides or dense woods". Grand buildings include Mr Darcy's home in the 2005 film adaptation of *Pride and Prejudice* in the form of Chatsworth House in Bakewell, down the road from Sheffield. The lovely town of Buxton similarly nestles in there, a place I visited as a teen with my friend and her mum, inexplicably overexcited that I could drink the water straight out the fountain in the town square. Also worth a mention in the Staffordshire part of the Peaks is Alton Towers, a theme park I have been to countless times growing up, doing the loop-the-loop until I regurgitated my chips.

Back up north and over to the east, Yorkshire is home to

both the Dales and the Moors. If you're confused between the two, for the former think hilly, for the latter think *Wuthering Heights*. According to Martha in *The Secret Garden*, the moors are "none bare" being "covered wi' growin' things as smells sweet". The Moors hover over York and extend to the coast encircling Robin Hood's Bay, a fishing village named after the Prince of Thieves who, according to folklore, defended the inhabitants from French pirates. Simon Armitage described a trip there where he joined a pub quiz after having fish and chips on the beach alongside dive-bombing seagulls. Sounds like a pretty Northern way to pass an evening to me.

The Dales start above Leeds and loom over Lancashire. The first time I went was in 2009 when some university friends and I went hiking to Malham Cove and the heavens drizzled on us the entire way, making the twelve thousand-year-old curved limestone formations particularly slippery buggers to walk on. But the trip was still beautiful, and we saved a sheep from a ditch which was pretty exciting. Cumbrian poet Norman Nicholson described the area as being "where flinty clints are scraped bone-bare/ A whale's ribs glint in the sun." If you're a *Harry Potter* fan, you may recognise the distinctive location from the *Deathly Hallows* film (the scene where HP and Hermione ditch Ron and mope about in a tent-with-a-view). The last time I went was 2023 when I strolled around the Fewston and Swinsty reservoirs, north of Otley. But the place I've been countless times is Ilkley Moor, at the bottom of the Dales and an easy drive from Leeds. With great views, you can wander amongst heather and water trickling over rock and, if you're eagle-eyed, find one of Simon Armitage's Stanza Stones.

If you're that way inclined, you can rise to the Yorkshire Three Peaks challenge which consists of twenty-four miles and one-thousand five-hundred-and-eighty-five metres of incline over the summits of Pen-y-Ghent, Whernside, and

Ingleborough in under twelve hours. The Peaks form part of the Pennines, the hills and mountains separating the Northeast from the Northwest (my dad likes to joke that they were put there by Lancashire people to keep Yorkshire folk out). Poet Sally Evanz described the North Pennines as green flesh on white rock bones, and it's this grassy body that Manc writer, Anita Sethi, decided to walk across to reclaim her attachment to the land she calls home after receiving racist abuse on a train and being told to "go home". On proposing her book about this journey, a Londoner told her that no-one cares about the North and advised not to talk about the Pennines as it wouldn't sell. Turns out they were wrong, as she was nominated for a nature writing award for the book.

But it's not all rolling hills for tourists and ramblers. Hannah Hauxwell gained fame in the 1970s for her appearance in documentaries about traditional farming in harsh Northern winters. Of the life, she declared: "In summer I live, in winter I exist", often going ten days at a time without seeing anyone and living without running water or electricity. Raised in a remote Dales farm, after other family members had passed, she managed eighty acres alone, battling prejudices of the time being the sole female farmer of the land. In one documentary, the baritone male narrator informed viewers that the white-haired woman "has never had a man in her life." The 'Daughter of the Dales' quite reasonably explained that a good marriage cannot compare to being alone, but that sharing a space with "someone you feel at variance with" is "horrible". Plus, you can't just walk into a shop and ask for a husband, she added. After years of hard work, she moved to a cottage in the '90s, leaving behind what is now a nature reserve named Hannah's Meadow.

Another stretch of land preserved for our benefit is the 73-mile reach of Hadrian's Wall, a World Heritage Site marking the historic division of Roman Britannia with the unconquered

Caledonia further north. Spanning Cumbria, Northumberland, and Tyne and Wear, the trail snakes over hills with stunning views either side of the wall. Tragically, in 2023 two men saw fit to fell the 200-year-old tree that stood iconically in the Sycamore Gap. The National Trust collected what was left and, a year later, seeds from the tree began to grow.

From Roman forts to Norman castles, south from the eastern side of the wall in County Durham sits Barnard Castle, a place that Boris Johnson's senior advisor, Dominic Cummings, brought to even greater prominence. During the height of lockdown when the rest of us were ordered to stay home, he apparently went to "test his eyesight" (no, seriously, that was his excuse) in the pretty little town named after the castle it's built around. In a humorous move by a cheeky lot even further north, the Scottish-founded company BrewDog released a 'hazy' beer called Barnard Castle Eye Test, with all proceeds going towards producing hand sanitiser for the NHS.

In addition to choosing your moments to visit wisely, you also have to select your towns carefully. My sister wanted to book a weekend away with her partner for their anniversary and remembered that our parents had recommended the quaint town of Berwick-upon-Tweed, the northernmost town in England before you hit Scotland that has actually changed hands between the two countries fourteen times throughout history. Over a family dinner, she asked them to remind her what Barrow-in-Furness was like because she'd booked and wanted to get excited. "You mean Berwick-upon-Tweed?" my mum asked? She did not. Instead of being sympathetic, my mum laughed and broke the news that there was nothing at Barrow but an old shipyard. My dad helpfully explained that it was "like Birkenhead before it got rejuvenated," adding cheekily, "I spent a week there one weekend and have no desire to ever return." To be fair to my sister, as a kid I would get Stoke-on-Trent and Stratford-upon-Avon mixed up, and even writing this story I nearly wrote Burton-on-Trent instead of Berwick-upon-Tweed. Darn those pesky hyphenated towns. To be fair to Barrow, they ended up in a nice hotel on the outskirts of the town and legged it to a nearby National Trust nature reserve for the day.

If you can remember their names right, attractive little towns can be found across the North. As an undergraduate student, I interned at a local magazine in Wetherby, writing about nearby areas of interest in West Yorkshire such as Pontefract and Shibden and then, on returning to Leeds as a postgraduate, I befriended a group of international students so I could crash their weekend jaunts to hippy Hebden Bridge and seafront Filey. And since Leeds keeps drawing me back in, my most recent return to live in the city took me to Ilkley to meet a childhood friend who now works for Leeds United. On the way back from coffee and cake I stopped off at the Cow and Calf Rocks on Ilkley Moor to soak up the atmosphere and the view over the town. Enjoying a leisurely drive back to Leeds via the winding back lanes of the moor, I could appreciate signs asking motorists to slow down for crossing ducks, as well as an ambulance which was actually a Land Rover, I assume to navigate the twists and turns of those skinny hill roads.

We also have quaint cities in the likes of Lancaster, Durham, York, and Chester. Some claim Durham's cathedral is a masterpiece – Bill Bryson fell in love with it and it was used for filming some part of Hogwarts – though I'd agree with Stuart Maconie that once you've seen one big cathedral, you've kind of seen them all. I heard Bryson give a speech there as Durham University Chancellor at my sister's graduation, the most interesting part in an otherwise monotone afternoon in the cold cathedral. Also, I am biased since I grew up going to Chester cathedral, tracing the mosaics along the walls with my fingers and gaping at the

stained-glass windows. I also sang in my primary school choir teacher's wedding there, so I have a soft spot for it over other big, draughty places of Christian worship.

The name 'Chester' comes from Old English meaning 'Roman fort'. In the eighteenth century, Scottish author James Boswell wrote that "Chester pleases my fancy more than any town I ever saw" and apparently thought the ladies were "charming". With its Roman walls, Norman Cathedral, and Tudor streets, it isn't half bad. I remember visiting a friend in Boston and a walking tour proudly showed off its three-hundred-year-old buildings. That's sweet, I thought. My hometown has two millennia of architectural history with a number of five-hundred-year-old pubs kicking about. I used to work in a relatively old one – Ye Olde Custom House – a seventeenth century Grade II listed building and one of the first pubs the race-goers hit coming into town. The oldest pub in the city, The Blue Bell Inn, was built in 1494 though is now firmly in the twenty-first century as a tapas bar. It is, of course, haunted, as you don't knock about for that long without racking up a number of lost souls.

Chester's black and white buildings are also home to 'The Rows', a two-tiered shopping experience with a covered upper level, unique to the country and dating back to the Tudor era.

The Victorians later decided monochrome timber was back in and tried to recreate the style so there are some sneaky mock Tudor houses in there too. The River Dee was also the reason the Romans set up camp there (though Liverpool was pretty happy when it silted up, making them the most important port instead). And we even have a castle; granted, a small one that is hardly ever open to the public, overlooking the racecourse which is the oldest still in operation in England having been founded in 1539. We are also very proud of our Roman amphitheatre, though if you've been to Rome's colosseum or seen the aqueduct in Seville, our pile of rocks in the ground might fail to impress.

Our town hall has a clock tower with only three faces, the blank side facing Wales, 'cos we're petty like that. We're also pretty protective of our territory as there exists to this day an archaic law permitting the shooting of a Welshman found within the city walls after midnight. But only with your bow and arrow, mind. Luckily no one has tested whether this defence would hold up in court today. We're also one of the few walled cities left in England today, along with York, my second favourite city with its rambling Shambles – originally christened the Great Flesh Shambles due to housing a load of butcher shops. (Another for the *Harry Potter* fans, the Shambles provided inspiration for Diagon Alley, with its narrow streets and overhanging timber frames). The city's shortest street is eloquently named Whip-ma-Whop-ma-Gate, which apparently comes from 'neither whit not what street' in old English meaning 'neither this nor that', which is a great street name if you ask me.

Outside of the county town, Cheshire has many other places of natural beauty, though the landscape is not typically Northern. No wild moors or great hills with stone walls criss-crossing them, instead rolling plains full of dairy farms with hedgerows partitioning the land like a patchwork quilt. When a friend of mine from London visited, as we turned off the motorway and past the first farmlands, she declared that it smelled like shit. "Welcome to the countryside!" I told her, cheerfully. The village where I grew up – and where my sister returned to raise her kids – is surrounded by farming hamlets, has an old Roman street creatively named 'The Street', and two pubs on either side of the river so that when it flooded back in the day, travellers on either side could wait until the following morning to continue their journey. I guess it used to rain a lot because our local church is situated on a hill that, according to legend, a man pledged to build after he floated away in a flood and prayed that he would honour the next land he came across with a place of worship.

During the pandemic, I took it upon myself to explore every nook and cranny of my local area, and what pretty nooks I found. From the waterfront along the Wirral to the castles of Beeston and Peckforton, the stately homes of Lyme and Tatton Park, and the forest of Delamere, I am happy to report that I never got bored. Granted, there was nothing else to do, but I stand by their subtle beauty. Helsby Hill has wide views of rural Cheshire, the hills of North Wales and even Liverpool on a good day (you just have to excuse the power plant, chemical works, and Bic factory that tar the view a bit). You can also just about see Beeston Castle, whose three-sixty view on the other hand has no industrial blemishes on its horizon. As a teen, I once snuck in after dark with friends and slept on a rock face which was both uncomfortable and inconducive to rest as I worried I'd roll off the edge in my sleep. The sunrise from that ledge was amazing though. The nearby Peckforton castle hosted a friend's fairy-tale wedding, but also has a steep public footpath through forest up and over the castle's hill if you are not so fortunate to be invited inside.

As well as being a salt county (the 'wich' in towns such as

Nantwich and Northwich indicate a saltwater spring), Cheshire is sometimes referred to as the 'Surrey of the North' and boasts the most money donated to charity across the country. This is less surprising when you consider the so-called 'Golden Triangle', made up of three of the most affluent towns and villages of the North, possibly the country. According to *The Independent*, only Mayfair has more millionaires per capita than Wilmslow. This blew my mind, having spent eighteen years down the road and having no inkling of this goldmine. I couldn't have pointed to it on a map or told you which direction to drive in. I thus felt it my duty while writing this to go in search of the mysterious place: like the Bermuda triangle, except instead of being hard to get out of, this one's hard to get into. This corner of Cheshire once housed landed gentry and mill owners looking to escape the big smoke and, whilst a couple of the villages retain this population, others have become peppered with footballers, TV soap stars, and other members of the *nouveau riche*. Wilmslow falls into the former category where, according to Jennings, "the comfortably heeled Mancunian lives when he's not setting up country club leisure facilities in the Algarve or helping to export bathware fittings in Lagos."

Before heading over there, I decided to watch *The Real Housewives of Cheshire* – for anthropological purposes, of course, and to help me blend in so as not to get arrested while cruising round the villages peering into people's homes. What I discovered was obligatory catfights in broad accents buried in a sea of fake tans. And fake lips and nails and eyebrows and hair and probably boobs, though I didn't stare (actually, I did, and they didn't move so I'm going with fake). So, off I went to investigate and, passing walkers or joggers, I had to restrain myself from rolling down the window to inquire if they were a millionaire or not. Lucky for them, the pandemic meant I wasn't allowed near anyone anyway, so I continued my trip to Alderley Edge. Driving first through Wilmslow I was a bit underwhelmed by the high street as I expected it to be dripping in gold but obviously the mansions were tucked away amongst the fields, the centre reserved for the plebs in their semi-detached houses. Nevertheless, a quick look online at the house prices in the area showed a two-bed flat for £400,000 but for a mere £3m you can get a detached six-bed house. I started to see some convertibles, which became a recurring sight throughout my afternoon, as well as a spattering of Range Rovers and an Aston Martin showroom. Alderley Edge's high street was much prettier, though they still had normal stuff like chippies and bus stops and charity shops (though I hear they're full of designer garb that is priced at five hundred instead of five thousand).

Having seen enough of how the other half live, at Alderley Edge I hopped on a walk which took me through a forest with gnarled trees growing in every direction, a perfect playground for kids. Since I had no kids with me, I honoured my inner child by climbing up a particularly sturdy-looking tree, though I can report that I didn't make it very far and ripped my jeans on the way back down. Children have a combination of flexibility and fearlessness which I appear to have lost in my adulthood, despite daily yoga and international travel. The walk offered a range of trails, though I declined the Miner's Path and chose the Wizard Walk – a nod to the area's Merlin legend – which took you past a cheerful Wizard Tea Room tucked not too inconspicuously in the woods near the car park, then up a gentle hill with impressive views of the Peak District and, I hear, the Pennines on a good day. Just outside the woods I came across a more upmarket Merlin Restaurant, beautifully decorated and, I imagine, beautifully priced.

A detour through Prestbury took me to the final village in the Triangle, on whose back lanes I found the kind of houses I'd been expecting. I could practically hear my mum grumbling about how footballers are paid too much while shaking her bob. Family bonding often includes my dad and I whinging about how much money the Royal Family get, and we can't drive past the Duke of Westminster's estate without someone tutting about how much of Chester they own.

A friend of mine said we had instilled in her a kind of disdain for privilege which made it hard transition from our run-of-the-mill comprehensive school to a private institute for Sixth Form. I would say that's quite a Northern attribute, handed down through generations of anti-establishment, working-class DNA. Nevertheless, I still like going to stately homes to see how the upper classes used to live and so often join my sister and brother-in-law on their National Trust adventures (they are resigned to the fact that membership means they are now official grown-ups). Last year we went to Tatton Park and they watched with trepidation as I tried to get as close to the deer as possible, but had to settle on watching a dog show, as the former didn't seem keen on me joining their herd. We then took my niece to Lyme Park so she could meet some more deer, but polite yet firm notices asked us not to go into their reserve, so that idea had to be abandoned. We also failed at finding Mr Darcy's lake because it started to rain (remember drippy Colin Firth stood in front of Pemberley?) but we did get great views of the Peak District and a hazy city in the distance we took to be Manchester.

On the other side of Cheshire lies the Wirral, a fifteen-mile-long peninsula where you can find the model village of Port Sunlight, built in 1899 by Bolton-born William Lever to house his three thousand five hundred factory employees. The village included allotments, a hospital, schools, a concert hall, a swimming pool, a church, an art gallery named after Lady Lever, and a temperance hotel. Lever wanted to "socialise and Christianise business relations" arguing that profits were shared via investment in the village. He apparently claimed "it would not do you much good if you send it down your throats in the form of bottles of whisky, bags of sweets, or fat geese at Christmas. On the other hand, if you leave the money with me, I shall use it to provide for you everything that makes life pleasant – nice houses, comfortable homes, and healthy recreation." A tad patronising, but at least he was a benevolent overlord. The village even became the setting for a 1912 West End musical comedy called *The Sunshine Girl* about a factory worker who falls in love with the heir to the 'Sunshine' soap factory in a typical case of star-crossed lovers.

Other claims to fame include the fact that Ringo Starr made his official debut there in 1962 (though by the time this happened I reckon the alcohol ban might've been lifted). Now it's simply a pleasant village to walk around. The gallery, open to the public, explores the darker side to the village in Lever's links to slavery in the Belgian Congo after the Lever Brothers leased land from infamous King Leopold II.

A similar endeavour had been established in 1851 just outside of Bradford in a workers' village (also publess) called Saltaire, named after its founder, Sir Titus Salt. Ironically, and perhaps somewhat irreverently, there is now a brewery named Saltaire in nearby Shipley. I visited in 2021 and, once you get past Shipley, it's pretty quaint with its cobbled streets, river, and local bakery. Saltaire's Club and Institute had a library, reading room, and lecture programme where residents met to discuss the anti-slavery movement, parliamentary reform, and presentations on travel. Women's suffrage meetings were also held there with Salt's daughter, Isabel, also giving speeches. When I was there, I peeked inside the Hall and it was still in use with a school production of something in full practising swing. Nothing political, as far as I could tell, but chock full of disco lights to make up for it.

Back along the River Mersey you can find parkland built

on what used to be a tip, transformed into nature reserves with great views across the estuary towards the Liverpool skyline, with its iconic Radio City tower and competing cathedral silhouettes. A couple more stops on the train takes you to Rock Ferry where a friend of mine lived (or, as some ironically refer to it, *Roush Farrer*, like when people call Primark *Primarché*). When I typed "is Rock Ferry..." to see if it belonged to Cheshire or Merseyside, the first autofill suggestion was "rough". When I clicked on it out of interest, the first article was "Rock Ferry – Worst places to live in Britain." Not just England, which you could argue is impressive. There have been many government housing schemes to reinvigorate the area so, for affordable home ownership in these times, I know worse places to live; especially when you get to be so close to a body of water.

If you took a ferry across the Mersey (did the song pop into your head?) you might see the *Titanic* memorial to the engine-room crew from Merseyside who lost their lives. The Merseyside Maritime Museum tells of the city's links to the doomed vessel, such as Fred Fleet, the *Titanic*'s Liverpudlian lookout who spotted the iceberg and said that if he'd been given binoculars the disaster might never have occurred. Seems like a bit of an oversight, but then hindsight is a wonderful thing. Fleet suffered from depression and hung himself in 1965, fifty-three years after the *Titanic* sank. As succinctly uttered towards the poor lad in James Cameron's 1997 film version: "Smell ice, can ya? Bleedin' Christ!"

Along the Liverpool coastline lies a series of Anthony Gormley sculptures called 'Another Place' (the same artist of 'Angel of the North' fame and, though he's not Northern, we seem to like his work). Gormley can be seen in all his naked metal glory one hundred times over Crosby beach when the tide is out. It's not the prettiest beach but it's always nice to be near water, and I'm sure the local economy is happy with

Gormley's multiple appendages which draw tourists in for a photo opp. That said, when my sister and I went during low tide to see the statues, quicksand was a real issue. Not as bad as at Morecambe where many a horse and cart were known to have disappeared crossing the sands, conjuring images of Bastian's horse in *Neverending Story*, but you still don't want to get your ankles stuck in it. Perhaps fittingly, the name 'Liverpool' comes from an Old English word meaning 'sludge'. This part of the coastline is also where you can find the Sefton coast, home to the largest undeveloped dune system in the UK with over twenty-two miles of sand dunes, providing a welcome habitat to a number of rare plant and animal species including the Merseyside sand lizard, the natterjack toad, and the north dune tiger beetle. Maybe they like the sludge.

About fifty miles north along the western coast is Lytham St. Annes, a town so posh the seagulls fly upside down, according to my auntie. A further forty or so miles north you'll find Morecambe, whose name derives from the Celtic meaning 'sea bay'. My grandma lived not far from the bay for twenty years before she moved back to Rawtenstall, so we used to go every time we visited as kids. Morecambe Bay (thus, Sea Bay Bay) was once a fashionable seaside resort but now has that all-too-common feel of a run-down coastal has-been. I still loved going though, mainly because of Happy Mount Park, a garish but thoroughly enjoyable theme park that is now closed after a stint as a Mr Blobby-themed world called Wrinkly Bottom in the '90s. I can't imagine what went wrong.

Morecambe's wide bay spans from Lancashire to Cumbria and may look pretty but has a tide that can sneak up on you and wash you clean away. In 2004, this occurred when twenty-one undocumented Chinese cockle pickers were taken out onto the Bay by inexperienced Merseyside father and son overseers who made a mistake about the times of the tides. To avoid such tragedies, Morecambe has its own queen-appointed guide to lead people across the six mile walk of the Bay in summer when the tide's out. It's still on my 'to do' list as, the last time I attempted it, it lashed down so hard we settled on doing the shorter four-mile round trip to Chapel Island, where you can observe nesting birds from a respectful distance. I can report that I finished the walk covered pretty much head-to-toe in sand slush, helped in large part by the numerous dogs on the walk that I felt compelled to say "hi" to every time they hurtled passed, unphased by the damp weather. During the pandemic a *Daily Mash* article reported that on Morecambe Sands: "Everyone was distancing, greeting each other with a polite tip of the hat and taking their rubbish home with them", whilst Bournemouth beach was rammed with people which, according to the article, delighted Northerners as it proved "once and for all that Southerners are just scum with fancy accents."

Morecambe used to compete with Blackpool for best west coast seaside town, the distance between the two being 42 miles, as the crow flies. Tatt-tastic Blackpool with its imitation Eiffel Tower was immensely popular with folks from the mill towns who saved up for months to go, one Burnley man explaining how "everything was costed to the last penny. If you went to a show on the pier, and was charged twopence for something instead of the expected penny, then your holiday plans were thrown askew. You would be hard up by the weekend!" Fast-forward to the noughties and Maconie described Blackpool as "chip fat and sodium lights... fizzy keg lager, the crash of slot machine and Robbie Williams." Birthing the world's first Big Dipper rollercoaster in 1921, Blackpool Pleasure Beach and illuminations have drawn many a family over the years; it's a place most kids from Lancashire grew up going to, and both coastal areas allegedly used to attract more visitors than the stunning beaches of Greece. With a potentially murderous tide and a high likelihood of rain this may be hard to imagine, but that is what I've been told happened before cheap Ryanair flights.

Modern Blackpool has since lost some of its appeal, attracting mostly hen dos and stag nights, L-plates askew, blow-up dolls ending life discarded in a roadside puddle somewhere. Charles Jennings unflinchingly called it a "town that could drive any sane person mad" full of "white trash holidaymakers". That said, he's not alone in his analysis, as seen in a tweet sent during the first pandemic lockdown by "queer peer educator" Stevie Boebi: "I can't believe I sold all of my belongings and left my dream house in Los Angeles to travel Europe and now for six months I'll be stuck in Blackpool, England." Condolences friend, but it could be worse, you could be stuck in Luton. No seaside there.

The Sheffield-born London-living friend of mine reckons that the North has nicer beaches than the South anyway. The beaches closest to Chester growing up weren't up to much. Rhyl in North Wales, once a thriving beach town, could be found dotted with needles and used condoms in my youth. Undiscouraged, as soon as I got my first car, a 1995 turquoise Rover Metro called Betty, I'd head to the beach with my mates to have a chippy tea on our knee, greasy-fingered and fending off fearless seagulls at West Kirby or New Brighton on the Wirral. I'm not sure if my mate has ever been to Cornwall (I haven't but I hear top reviews) but she mentioned two beaches she rated: Scarborough – the east's answer to Blackpool – and Flamborough Head, an eight-mile stretch of cliff-lined coast in Yorkshire which has seals and puffins and the occasional dolphin or whale (though they were all hiding when I went).

Once Covid vaccines had been rolled out across the country and the pandemic was starting to feel like a collective bad dream, a friend of mine bought a van and asked me if I wanted to take a road trip with her to test it out. I of course said "yes", and we decided to head beach-wards. Already in Leeds at that time, Rach headed over from Manchester to scoop me up in her new acquisition, Van Berlin, destination Scarbados, ending at her new pad in Whitley Bay. On the way, we took a trip down memory lane listening to the pop punk tunes we grew up on along the way, then Maximo Park's 'The Coast is Always Changing' on repeat as soon as we saw the sea. I suggested a route stopping at Malton, Yorkshire's food capital, where we swung in to fill our bellies with some afternoon scones (and the driver's bloodstream with caffeine). The town is small but perfectly formed with some great little shops and cafés, a small museum about how Malton became the area's breadbasket due to its river access in the early 1700s, later becoming known for brewing up a beery storm in the 1800s. In true Yorkshire style, the main square also has a recipe for Yorkshire puddings painted on the side of a building.

Feeling refreshed and pleased with our first discovery, we continued our journey pointing Vanny B at Robin Hood's Bay where we stopped for a pint-with-a-view and then rolled on down to the beach. Despite it being freezing and windy with dark rain clouds rolling ominously in, Rach donned a wetsuit and got in the sea whilst I sat on the sand and scribbled badly-written poetry. When the water in the leaden clouds insisted on re-joining the North Sea, we hauled ourselves back up the hillside and carried on our journey to Scarborough.

Brollies at the ready, we walked down to the seafront, past the donkeys and the shops selling colourful rock (I bought my dad one saying 'Old Fart'), and into the doorway of an amusement hall. We both love the penny pusher arcade games, so messed about with those for a while (and came out 20p up, thank you very much). Getting peckish, we peered in about ten chippies before settling on one we liked the look of, The Tunny Club. Tucked into a side street off the main drag, the inside is covered in historical photos and newspaper clippings about the area such as the first woman to break a fish catching record, and so on. They call themselves 'world renowned' and, though I'm sure if I drop the name the next time I'm outside of the UK I'll get blank stares, it was some good grub deserving of a mention.

Then, despite it being the height of summer, England did what England is so good at, opening the heavens upon us so we decided to look for somewhere to shelter indoors as we didn't fancy a night of being soggy in the van. It just so happened that the Grand Scarborough Hotel (which Rach's mate affectionately nicknamed the Grotty Grand) had an offer on. Once claiming to be the largest brick structure in Europe, Winston Churchill stayed there, as did Anne Brontë, though the sea air could not save her, as she shuffled off the mortal coil in that very spot. More recently it was one of the hotels that housed Afghan refugees after the Taliban returned in 2021, and that day it was giving us refuge from the lashing rain. It turned out the nightly bingo was cancelled (very disappointing and we couldn't seem to convince the girl behind the bar to step up: "All you have to do is read out numbers?") but there was still entertainment on at 9.54pm. To kill time, we decided to take drinks to our room and watch *The Shining* (it seemed appropriate). Just as Jack Nicholson was dragging an axe up the stairs, a man knocked on our fifth-storey window, having climbed over the balcony to teeter on the small stone ledge. Needless to say, it scared the shit out of us. My mate repeatedly informed me: "There's-a-man-at-the-window-there's-a-man-at-the-window!" whilst hitting my leg under the duvet. I replied, with amazing thinking in a panic: "Don't make eye contact, maybe he'll go away", thinking he was a drunk creeper trying to get us to climb back to his room to party with him. Turns out I was a little off, cos he then announced: "I'm gonna throw meself off." Rach leapt out of bed, heading to the window: "Oh right, OK mate," then growl-whispering to me: "Call the police!" I'd already grabbed my phone and, while I called emergency services, she shouted through the window asking if he wanted to talk. By the time we'd figured out how to open the window a few inches (it's sealed well shut for a reason) he'd hopped on over to let the next poor sods know of his plans. As if in our own kind of surreal movie, while the police attempted to talk him in from the next room, we went to watch "the turn" (it was 9.45 by then) which consisted of four sequinned young women prancing about singing '60s classics to a hall that was probably less than a quarter full. A policewoman came to have a nosey too. But all's well that ends well as, by the time we went to bed, the fire trucks had gone and there was no white chalk body outline on the ground outside.

The next day we decided a soggy van might be the best bet after all, but had yet to find a place to park Van for the night as everywhere was fully booked. Starting to worry (or at least I was, Rach is very laid back about these things) we tried looking at campsites further inland. Success finally came at a site on the Yorkshire Moors, so we set off just in time for the pelting rain to begin again. Let's just say I was 100 per cent glad I wasn't driving, but nonetheless scared that my friend was, as she ragged Van Berlin around slippery bends in poor visibility. When the clouds relented, the drive over the Moors was beautiful, purple heather clinging to the fells as far as the eye could now gleam, then it was up down up down over winding country lanes until we reached the site.

We were greeted by a great white Barn Owl, wings outstretched, on the hunt for prey as dusk closed in, which we took to be a good omen. As Van was yet to be converted into a habitable space, we set about blowing up the bed and hanging fairy lights to make it cosy and, once we'd unfolded the table and cracked open a bottle of red, we tried to play cards without getting drizzled on or attracting too many insects. We failed at the latter tasks but, much to my friend's delight, we did get the following comment from two ten-year-old boys passing by: "Mate, that van is sick".

Despite the lulling rain patter on the roof, I had a rubbish night's sleep as Rach is a bed-hogger, we were parked on a slight incline so I kept rolling into the cold, damp, metal inside of the van and, without windows in it, I was convinced I was going to suffocate to death in the night. After knocking up some scrambled eggs, we went for a wander around the site to wake up then decided to squeeze in one more coastal visit because Rach loves the water and I love books and the supernatural.

Whitby sits nestled into the coastline, the port protected by the curving edges of the land. We got yet more fish and chips (which weren't as good, so I generously shared my chips with a seagull who was being uncharacteristically polite about asking for some) and then headed up the hill – 199 steps, to be precise – to Whitby Abbey, a ruined Benedictine abbey immortalised by Bram Stocker's *Dracula*. Thirsty after all our touristing, we parked ourselves in the brew pub opposite the abbey and enjoyed some local beer with an atmospheric view. There also happened to be a miniature train festival in a nearby field so we got a parade of the neat locomotives passing by intermittently. On our way back, I picked up some obligatory vampire-themed stick rock that I knew I'd never eat but that brought me some fleeting joy.

The sun came out for an hour so we made a quick stop in the lovely fishing village of Staithes (whose claim to fame is being where Captain Cook first tested out his sea legs) and treated ourselves to some ice cream by the port. We then left Yorkshire and headed to the Northeast to Seaham where I'd heard there was a beach filled with sea glass pebbles. The internet photos were somewhat misleading as we only managed to scrounge a couple of tiny shards after an hour of digging but, as we told ourselves, an hour by the sea is better than an hour not by the sea, sea glass or no sea glass.

Our last stop was Beamish, "the living museum of the North" which, if you haven't been, I recommend arranging a trip now. Set in large grounds in countryside near Durham, it recreates towns and villages from the area in the eighteen- and nineteen-hundreds. And you don't just wander around looking at stuff, you go in houses, buy bread from the bakery, get yelled at by a Mrs Trunchbull lookalike in school and go down a real coal mine, the latter experience narrated by an animated five-foot man in a flat cap. He told us all about the horrific conditions – a standout fact being that the men had to "do their business where they lay" once nestled horizontally between rock and coal. Thousands of pit ponies spent their entire lives down there, never to see daylight again.

The rain had turned to a light drizzle, the kind that still manages to soak to you the bone, so we decided to spend our last night at Rach's, since Whitley Bay was just as close as finding another campsite to squelch about in. This meant that the last night of our trip was spent with my mate's cat pawing at my face from the crack of dawn, but at least we were dry. Ending the trip officially sleep-deprived, I was still highly entertained on the train back from Newcastle to Leeds when an announcement asked passengers to put knee-high suitcases on the rails overhead and leave space for the bigger suitcases – unambiguously described as "the ones you could put a body in" – in the racks by the doors.

All in all, and in spite of the rain, it was a cracking trip that I would highly recommend, showing what you can do with a long weekend. Also, don't tell my family this but, having traversed the countryside and coast of North Yorkshire, I now understand why they claim it as God's country.

And I might have to agree.

V. There's Nowt So Queer as Folk

Nah then, it in't proper to talk about the North for so long and not give a nod of our flat caps to its accent and dialect. There's a hilarious song by Latin American brothers Juan Andrés and Nicolás Ospina about how difficult it is to learn Spanish because if you move countries, the changes in dialect will trip you up left, right, and centre. I'd argue the same can be said for moving ten miles down the road in England.

Bill Bryson explained in his book, *Mother Tongue*, "if we define dialect as a way of speaking that fixes a person geographically, then it is scarcely an exaggeration to say that in Britain there are as many dialects as there are hills and valleys." He goes on to describe how, in a town bordering both Lancashire and Yorkshire, people reckon they can tell which side of the street you were born on by your accent – something my mother has long argued. It baffles me that Mancunians and Liverpudlians sound so different. It seems like they should be separated by a good hundred miles. In fact, it's about thirty, though both cities used to be part of Lancashire, so how Liverpool ended up sounding so distinct is beyond me. Greater Manchester and Cheshire are separated by the Manchester Ship Canal, Lancashire and Yorkshire by the Pennines, but Greater Manchester and Merseyside merge into one another with no notable geographic divide. So what happened? Locals susceptible to foreign sailors' and traders' accents? Irish immigration? Scouse stubbornness to set themselves apart? Whatever the reason, I love its uniqueness.

Across Lancashire's mill towns, each has their own accent. According to W.R. Mitchell, Oldham speech is "reet in the mouth, flopping about", whilst Rochdale is "rounded vowels, pushed up in the mouth". Wiganers, apparently, "chew their words." My own city of Chester has a hybrid accent; a product of in-migration from other counties. Of my high school friends, I can't name a single one whose parents are from Cheshire. Blackpool, Chorley, Manchester, Liverpool, Wrexham, London even – but not Cheshire. I eventually found someone with both sides of the family from Chester in my parents' next-door neighbour, whose great grandma was Cestrian and, before that, her family were Irish; an ancestry common to the Northwest. Apparently, the Chester accent is one of the easiest for Amazon's 'Alexa' contraption to understand across the UK (though witnessing my sister's attempts to communicate with it would say otherwise). I'd say that, depending on where your parents come from or who you hang out with, Chester folk fall somewhere between a more neutral (read, middle-class), Manc/Lanc, or Scouse brogue. If you fall into the latter, you might be considered unlucky as, whilst I like a Scouse accent, it seems others do not as a 2007 study found that the Liverpool accent was perceived to be the worst in England.

In my own family, my parents have a Lancashire tinge, softened by thirty-odd years in Cheshire, my sister has a scouse twang having knocked about with Birkenheaders (land of the true Scousers, apparently), and mine can't seem to make its mind up after ten years of moving around. As a result, I've been asked if I'm Scottish, Irish, Canadian, or, very specifically, from Devon. Though, if Americans' attempts to mimic my accent are anything to go by, I now sound like Dick Van Dyke or Keira Knightley. (I think that might be more to do with them than me.) Plus, as T. Thompson wrote in his 1945 book *Lancashire Pride*, I still "slip into dialect among friends like we slip into an old and comfortable coat when we reach home"; my own Northern tones re-emerging on sight of Helsby Hill.

My extended family, the rest of whom remain in Lancashire, talk a bit broader, like, to the point where, as a child, I sometimes had to ask my mum what my grandparents were saying. I was used to my parents asking if I was "born in a barn" when I left the door open but was stumped when my grandparents told me to "put wood in th' 'oil". Shuffling over to my mum, I asked what I was supposed to do in an uncertain whisper. She laughed and explained that I should shut the door (put the wood in the hole) and thus began my interest in dialect.

Alan Bennett has argued that "people in the North seem to me to enjoy their language... they enjoy the way they speak... People tend to imagine that a northern English is simply standard English with a sort of dirty dishcloth sort of accent... and it isn't. The actual structure of the sentences is different, the emphasis comes at the end of the sentence. I mean, they'll say 'He's not a bad looking feller is that.' They kind of invert things."

I myself love how language is passed on from generation to generation, with new words creeping in, some dying out and others spreading, as well as new vocabulary invented by creative youth; the kind I saw and marvelled at growing up. I was once sat listening to a presentation about a book club in Barcelona which supported groups of people such as immigrants or people who couldn't read to access the literary greats such as Shakespeare and Cervantes; what the presenter called 'high culture'. I remember being niggled by a feeling of elitism. As wonderful as it is for everyone to be able to experience these texts, I'd love to see more reading groups for highly educated upper-class folks to understand texts written in local dialects or immigrant culture. Some of the words created by Northerners are as inventive as Shakespeare. As Sylvia Corbridge argues: "A people who can speak of twilight as "th'edge o' dark", and the east as "morning side", are not without poetry in their souls." Yorkshire actor Patrick Stewart agrees, recalling how he was at a football match back home recently and asked a man what he thought of the game, to which he replied, "Eeh, it were like suppin' hot lead." Another line I love from the classic film *Billy Liar* is his mum chiding him not to be late for work, shouting, "you'll set off one of these days and meet yourself coming back!" How can you not love the playfulness and imagery in this kind of language?

In days gone by, Lancashire folk nearing the end of their lives could be heard to say: "Ah've woven me piece", and I once interviewed a retired Yorkshireman for a documentary and, talking of a nephew stationed in Ireland during the Troubles, he described how it had "bombed him back to the cradle." If that's not some tragic Shakespearean poetry, I don't know what is. As well as creativity, there's also a homeliness in Northern dialect. An old Music Hall song that was sung in dialect goes:

> *Call round any old time*
> *Mak thissen at home*
> *Put thi feet on the mantel-shelf*
> *Sit by the fire and help thiself*
> *I don't care if your pals*
> *Have left thi all alone*

Rich or poor, knock on the door
Make thiself at home.

But there are concerns that Northern dialects are dying out. Corbridge argues that while schoolgirls in the '50s would have said of their boyfriend, "isn't 'e smashin'?", her granny would have said he was "reet as a ribbin and as fain as a lad wi' a new sute of clooas an' a buttercake." Nowadays they'd probably say, "'e's dead fit, inne?" Perhaps we're losing some poetry as the years go on, though we are left with modern means of expressing ourselves, such as 'lamping' someone who's a wrong'un, or lending your brolly to 'our kid' cos he's a good egg. 'Angin' if you drank too much, so you 'ave a kip to sleep it off. Then there's being chuffed with summat proper mint like a sunny day to bronze your tages, but seeing your arse if someone's gone all radge. Buzzing if the gig had pure people at it, but gutted if you're feeling ruff as chuff the next day. And so on. So maybe dialect isn't dying, but evolving.

My all-time favourite Lancashire expression has to be "it's cracking t' flags" when the sun is hot enough to crack stone, one I will hang on to for dear life as I believe as many people as possible should benefit from this turn of phrase. When it was cracking t' flags at my grandma's in Kirkby Lonsdale we would go for a walk over t' crags, the rough rock protruding from grassy hills. I loved passing through the 'kissing gates' and stroking any sheep that would come close enough to let me. Back at the house, my grandma – a woman of infinite patience – would occasionally declare: "Stop your mitherin'!" (or moiderin') when we tugged on her apron too many times for a slab of her homemade chocolate cake before dinner, then mutter "you're addled..." as we'd skip off singing or dancing. Or my great auntie would peer across the Rossendale valley and sniff at the air: "'Appen it'll rain later." Or my best mate's Leyland-born dad would tell us to "stop playing silly buggers" when we would mess about in the house. My mum also once came out with "me belly thinks me throat's been cut" when she was hungry. I initially didn't believe her that this vivid imagery was a real expression, but then I heard some Geordie say it on *Our Friends in the North* so her reputation as a truth teller was restored. Another saying my mum grew up with, found in Lancashire and Yorkshire, is: "Where there's muck there's brass" (brass refers to money and muck to dirty jobs).

Other great expressions from my family include when my grandma would say "hells bells" in surprise or horror. (Said grandma was a former hairdresser so when I moved to Madrid and went looking for a new hair salon and came across one called Hells Bells, I knew it was the place for me.) An even sweeter way to exhort disbelief upon hearing news is to say "'ecky thump", a favourite amongst my Preston relatives; or "eeh, by gum" to add emphasis on both sides of the Pennines. More weird and wonderful expressions to come out of my family include, "she's giving you a good coat of looking at" if someone is staring at you; "have you cleaned your peggies?" to mean brush your teeth; and calling people "daft as a brush", though I never understood why brushes were dafter than any other household object. My dad also has a curious habit of saying "ta da" instead of "ta ra", as if he's proud of a recently completed magic trick rather than trying to say goodbye to someone. His mate, Lee, signs off with a "tatty bye", a phrase borrowed from his neighbour, the late Liverpudlian comedian Ken Dodd.

While there are expressions that may be less used today, some are surely worth preserving. For example, W.R. Mitchell asked an Accrington man about the expression "all a-flunters", which he was told meant "in a reet pickle". When asked for clarification, the mildly irritated man offered: "all mucked up." Another wonderful Lancashire saying I stumbled across on Pendle Hill was found in the corner of a tourist map. The quote read: "Gerrit spent. They dont pupockits i shrahds." I puzzled over this, trying to decipher its meaning by attempting to read it phonetically, still needing to ask my mum who, chuckling, offered the more standardised version of "you can't take it with you," meaning your money to the grave. I assume the sign makers left this gentle encouragement to mean 'spend it in the gift shop on witchy literature, New Age jewellery, or tacky mugs with supernatural puns printed on them'.

In the same way that Scousers change football to 'footy', electricity to 'lekkie' and so on, Lancastrians refer to things by size in that we have a 'big light' and a 'big coat'. "Can we put the big light on?" I would ask if my parents were watching telly when I wanted to read, causing my dad to grumble, "Oh aye, why don't you put t' outside light on while you're at it so t' birds can read, too!" You need your 'big coat' when it's cold, but you'd better take it coat off inside or you won't 'feel the benefit' when you go back outside. Is it any surprise then that my sister had three teddy bears as a kid, unimaginatively named Big Ted, Little Ted, and Medium Ted? In the Northwest, Manchester uses 'cock' as an affectionate term, the equivalent of Yorkshire's 'love'. 'Chuddy' is used for chewing gum all the way from Cumbria to Cheshire, and Northerners often say 'scally' instead of 'chav', though in Tyneside they apparently say 'charva' or 'radgie'. Funnily enough, my sister and I both ended up being nicknamed 'scally', mine because it rhymes with my name and was ironic because I dressed more like a skater boy (think baggy Sohos, black eyeliner, and hair that regularly changed colour), hers because she was, well, a bit of a scal (think trackies, white eyeliner, and a slicked back ponytail with a very '90s fringe that defied gravity thanks to copious amounts of hairspray). Her other university housemate had the imaginative nickname 'Geordie' because he was, you guessed it, a Geordie.

In the Early Middle Ages, the marauding Vikings, in return for pillaging various villages and women in Yorkshire, left behind a glut of Norse words such as 'fell' for a hill and 'beck' for a stream. They also left a number of place names such as Duggelby which means the settlement of some Dug fellow, or Yockenthwaite, which refers to a clearing in a wood, and Grimwith which is a wood haunted by a ghost or goblin. Grimsby was named, according to a poem called *Lay of Havelock*, after a fisherman called Grim, who rescued a Danish king's son and not, contrary to popular belief, because someone visited and thought *blimey, this is grim*. Skipton, originally Shipton, had nothing to do with ships but a sheep farm. Another Nordic word found in both Yorkshire and the Northwest is 'shieling' which is a shepherd's shelter and the name of my childhood home, a nod to our family surname.

Charles Jennings astutely observed that Yorkshire seems to like place names beginning with the letter 'h' despite not pronouncing the thing: 'Aworth, 'Arrogate, 'Ebden Bridge, 'Alifax, 'Uddersfield, and 'Ull, to name a few. Aside from enjoying place names with letters they don't pronounce, the county has some great words such as 'brussen', referring to a kind of stubborn confidence. When I looked it up in the dictionary I found the following example: "He's a brussen sod, isn't he?" Brilliant. As well as stubbornness, another Northern quality is modesty. 'Showing off' is not encouraged, with those that thought they were better in my mother's village met with the disapproving expression "they think their pennies are tuppences" and my dad often told me not to be a 'smart Alec' if I ever answered back. Again, this is not uncommon across the North. Mark Hodkinson wrote that it was no good being "artsy or bookish in down-town, run-down Rochdale: who do you think you are? My parents feared I'd be bullied, picked off by the pack. By undermining me they believed they were helping me, saving me. They were adhering to a wider class code... There is also anti-intellectualism at work, as if they are afraid of you becoming clever in case you walk away, leave them behind." Carlisle writer, Grace Dent, says of trying acting at university that she realised why there so few working-class thespians as it was too "show-offy". It's one thing to be pretentious in the privacy of your own head, but certainly not in public. Finally, Liverpudlian director of the docudrama *Hillsborough*, Charles McDougall, explained: "particularly in the working-class North, the one thing you do not want is arrogance. That belongs to the South; the monied South. So the slightest sign of arrogance in your child, you knock it out of 'em." He goes on to reflect on the side effects of this worldview as, "in knocking out the arrogance you knock out the ambition, the self-respect, the self-esteem." Northern parents, take note.

Melvyn Bragg reported that in the 1950s, Northerners moving south felt they had to change their voice and vocabulary as those coming from "Hull or Preston or Pontefract" wouldn't be taken seriously. He interviewed a woman who recalled how her Canterbury colleagues had laughed at her when she said she was going to "wash the pots", though she hadn't got the joke. That was the 1970s and, as I listened some fifty years later, it was news to me that this was a Northern expression. When my mum was a child, my grandma sent her to elocution lessons so she wouldn't have as thick an accent as my grandma did, with the (not so crazy) assumption that it would give her a 'better chance in life'. Despite this investment, my mum says people in Cheshire still couldn't understand her, despite having only moved forty miles south. Continuing the tradition of smoothing out any accent – and by extension working-class signifiers – my mum would always correct me when I dropped my 't's. "Pass you the what? Bo'ul o' wa'er? Do you mean 'bottle of water'? Don't be lazy – pronounce your 't's," she would scold. I later learned that the sound was called a glottal stop and took pleasure in informing her that it was actually physically more effort than pronouncing a 't' so was thus not lazy (further entrenching my reputation as a Smart Alec). The glottal stop is a feature of the otherwise softer Northern accent found in Chester (and London for that ma'er). Yet despite not having a strong accent, the Southerners in Leeds would coo over my pronunciation of 'cup' and 'glass'; to which I would defensively retort that 'cap' is a different object and there's definitely no 'r' in glass.

My Southern friends were also highly entertained by the terms 'ginnel' and 'snicket' for an alleyway. My auntie, who lived just over the other side of Hadrian's Wall in Scotland, grew up in one of the back-to-back houses in Rawtenstall, using the ginnel down the middle as a cut through to avoid having to walk all the way around. Such houses were mostly demolished in the 1950 and '60s in a massive slum clearance to make room for the eyesore blocks of flats you can now see across the UK, although there are still some back-to-backs dotted around such as in my dad's hometown, Preston. Incidentally and according to legend, the word 'teetotal' was invented by a stuttering Prestonian who had allegedly gone into the equivalent of an A.A. meeting, plastered, to take the mickey out of the attendees, but ended up taking the pledge, declaring that "tha must be reet out and out abaht it. T...t...tee...total abstinence."

When living in Leeds, I used to take a train to stay with my grandma who would pick me up at the station, just over the Yorkshire border. We would play Scrabble, go charity shopping, and eat homecooked food. One particular visit, some classmates had accompanied me to explore the countryside, then I went to meet my grandma and they were going to return to the city. Upon hearing that my friends would be there, my great aunt wanted to come to "have a look at them" ('look' pronounced 'Luke' here) and, instead of waiting in the car as usual, the two women in their five-foot grandeur came shuffling over in their rain macs, expectant smiles on their faces. I hastily said my goodbyes to my friends and ushered the ladies back to the car. "Yer not embarrassed of us, are yer?" they asked. I didn't know how to answer. Was I embarrassed? Maybe. Or maybe I didn't want my Southern friends to patronisingly declare 'how cute' they were and mimic their accents.

Back then I was trying to make friends and didn't fully understand the history, politics, and power that came with an accent. As anyone from the Anglo-Celtic Isles will know, accents come with class associations. The 2022 series, *The Rings of Power*, caused outrage when the povviest hobbits were given atrocious 'Irish' accents, reflecting a pervasive assumption about regional speech. For example, that the less BBC the accent, the less privileged we assume someone to be. Or trustworthy, apparently. As expressed by Scot, Tom Leonard, in his poem *Six O'Clock News*:

> *thi reason*
> *a talk wia*
> *BBC accent*
> *iz coz yi*
> *widny wahnt*
> *mi ti talk*
> *aboot thi*
> *trooth wia*
> *voice lik*
> *wanna yoo*
> *scruff.*

When discussing the above with a friend, she protested that newsreaders do have Northern accents on BBC Northwest now. When I asked who, after some thought, she admitted that they were the sports and weather presenters. Not quite allowed to report the serious stuff (not that Brits don't take both sport and weather very seriously, but it's not the same). In Melvyn Bragg's podcast *Speaking from the North*, he asks a man with a broad accent to read the news. I swear it made me so happy I nearly cried. The power of hearing people who sound like they come from round your end has a subtle but deep affirming power.

As Stuart Maconie has pointed out, Radio 4 plays in which Northern voices feature are inevitably about 'being northern': "About how poor or cute or funny or indomitable we are. It will never simply be set in Sheffield or Hull or Wigan because it can be and it should be." Whilst there's nothing wrong with plays about being Northern, there doesn't appear to be a need for plays about being Southern because being Southern is the norm. That's what's referred to when talking about England (or worse, the UK) with images of thatched cottages, Oxbridge, and the Royal family conjured to mind.

During an interview with the Beatles at the beginning of their career, the interviewer asks if they will modify their Liverpool dialect for a Royal performance after some posh guy said he couldn't understand them as they didn't speak the 'Queen's English'. The boys turned the question around on the interviewer, saying "We wouldn't bother doin' that. We don't all speak like them BBC posh fellas, you know." In a fascinating turn of events, while the lads answered the rest of the questions in faux posh accents, the interviewer's accent appeared to soften (back to what was presumably his original Northern accent). Instead of bowing to the pressure to conform, they stood confidently in their Northern skin and made it cool to do so.

My mum tells a story of moving out of her native Rawtenstall for a secretarial job and her boss telling her months later: "When I interviewed you, I thought you were thick cos of your accent, but you're actually quite intelligent, aren't you?" In *Educating Rita*, a 1983 film about a working-class Liverpudlian who enrols on an Open University course, the namesake enters her tutor's office one day speaking exaggerated Queen's English. When the professor asks her why, she replies: "There's no point discussing literature with an ugly voice." She insists she is joking, but truth often lurks behind humour, reflecting an internalised belief that Northerners can't be intelligent if we sound like Nora Batty. Radio 4's *Woman's Hour* had a special episode for the fortieth anniversary of the play in 2020. Various women called in confirming that they could relate to the story, with one woman leaving her teacher training college after two days as she felt out of place among middle-class people and "felt stupid every time I opened my mouth" because of her broad Yorkshire accent. And if you think these are issues of yesteryear, 2018's *Jurassic World* film scripted a woman asking a child if she was a wild animal for saying "bath" instead of "baath" and telling her to use the Queen's English. In 2022, a theatregoer walked out of a play and demanded their money back after the actors performed Shakespeare in Yorkshire accents. The play was in a Yorkshire theatre. (Incidentally, Willy allegedly wrote a play in 1608 called *A Yorkshire Tragedy*, so it's not such a stretch for Shakesperean characters to sounds this way.) In defiance of such pushbacks, Bradford Opera Festival included a dialect opera in 2023, promoted as: "Eyup! Rossini's best loved comic opera put into proper Yorkshire" by poet Ian McMillan.

I also can't recall a single lecturer of mine in Leeds who spoke with a Northern accent, and this is, sadly, not an anomaly. A recent Durham University report produced by one local student on the 'Northern Student Experience' revealed a 'toxic attitude' towards students with a Northern twang. One Liverpudlian student reported needing counselling due to being reminded daily of her working-class background and another dropped out because of bullying that included mocking accents, jokes about coalminers, and accusations of theft and benefit-scrounging. Apparently "rolling in the muck" is used as a euphemism for sleeping with a Northern working-class person (excuse me while I vomit then choke on it in anger). Even to this day, I automatically 'code switch' when I talk in class, standardising my accent and avoiding saying things like "I thought the article wo'nt too bad, but the book we read was proper shit". Partly out of professionalism but then 'professionalism' is probably a bit classist (and racist/sexist) anyway.

A Northern mate of mine, while I was lamenting a lack of Northern accents in politics, said of Angela Rayner, "I know I shouldn't think this, but even I was shocked that she says all this intelligent stuff with that accent." How deep does this accent-class-intelligence yoke go? Rayner grew up on a council estate in Stockport, Greater Manchester, with a mother who couldn't read or write, and no qualifications herself after becoming pregnant at sixteen. She became an MP for Ashton-under-Lyme in 2015 then ran for, and successfully won, a position as deputy Labour leader in 2020 (as well as a place in my heart when she criticised parliament for being too "pale, male, and stale"). Running for the leadership was another Mancunian, Rebecca Long-Bailey, who argued that "you can't just put on a nice suit and be a bit suave and think that's a route into Downing Street." Apparently, you can because she lost out to Londoner Keir Starmer (a suave, posh-sounding, Oxbridge-educated white dude in a nice suit). Long-Bailey attended a Catholic school in my hometown and it seems our private schools have been churning out a few politicians of late as Cestrian, Health

Secretary Matt Hancock – the man responsible for communicating our clear-as-mud coronavirus strategy – attended an all-boys private school in Chester. On behalf of all Cestrians, we apologise for that one. Throughout the twentieth and twenty-first centuries, we have been led by Southerners, with the exception of Huddersfield's Harold Wilson who was Prime Minister with the Labour Party from 1964-1970 and 1974-1976. He would apparently drink bitter and smoke a pipe in public, man of the people, but smoke cigars and drink brandy in private.

Even in a satirical BBC Comedy sketch about trying to reframe the North as not being shit, Brennan Reece argued that: "Yeah, our accents are harsh, brash, and aggressive. But you should meet me nan – she makes my accent sound tepid." As well as dialect, it's also true that some accents are being diluted over time; mine a case in point. A recent study by the University of Manchester claimed that middle-class accents in Manchester, Sheffield, and Leeds are becoming more similar across regions, though Liverpool and Newcastle retain their distinctiveness. People may be relieved to hear the latter, as a Northern accent that people can not only tolerate but actually like is the Geordie one. Maconie argued that "the Samaritans love Geordie volunteers because their down-to-earth but quietly reassuring tones are proven to turn people's minds away from the gas oven and tablets." Thanks to Girls Aloud's Cheryl Cole, it was voted the UK's sexist accent in 2010 (I'm sorry to report that Bradford was voted third least sexy). Since then, however, the 2019 poll saw the Essex accent beating the Geordies to the top position thanks to 'reality' TV show, *The Only Way Is Essex*. In fact, Charles Jennings reckoned that Geordies were "everything southerners demand from northerners: poor sods with a derelict economy, glorious countryside, a nice line in self-deprecating humour and a wonderfully beguiling accent." Howay, man.

In 2016, a study by HSBC bank predicted that by 2066 the Brummie, Glaswegian, Scouse, Cockney, Mancunian, and Geordie accents will all be standardised as a result of "talking to machines and listening to Americans." It'd be a shame if forty years down the line we all sounded the same, as language and dialect help us communicate our cultural traditions. They carry within them the history and kinship that shaped them, and the humour and nature that defines us. If we lose that, we lose ways of thinking and interacting with one another, and our country loses some of its rich diversity. And I, for one, would like to keep that.

I'm not then only one either. Something I've noticed in Yorkshire recently is an embracing of local accents in company announcements, a refreshing and pleasing alternative to the usual go-to accent. When I moved back to Leeds in 2022 and called Yorkshire Water, the recording told me to "press two fer bills", so I did, with a nod of appreciation. I'd already noticed this a year earlier on a bus from Leeds to Saltaire as announcements were delivered to us by a man with a thick Yorkshire accent and, in 2023, Northern Rail took the decision to re-record 34 station name announcements to better reflect local pronunciation, such as Slaithwaite and Sowerby Bridge (pronounced "Slou-wit" and "Sowby"). I saw another attempt at reclaiming local accents on public transport on a recent trip to Hadrian's Wall, in a poster advert on the Settle-Carlisle line wishing us "'Appy travels". So it seems salvaging local ways of speaking has either become trendy, or companies have got wise to the fact that locals enjoy having their way of talking valued.

There is also an arena where any Northern accent can, for better or worse, be used in our favour. Entertainers are allowed to sound Northern, and perhaps are all the more amusing to others because of it. The Scousers had Cilla Black filling people's Fridays throughout the 1990s with *Blind Date*; Paul O' Grady gave us the blonde bombshell Lily Savage; and nowadays comedians like John Bishop and Chris McCausland grace the stage with their Liverpudlian presence. Bolton gave us Vernon and Peter Kay (unrelated), and Pete's mate Paddy McGuinness, who I warmed to after he dropped off a bunch of M&S sarnies at a Macclesfield hospital for NHS staff during the pandemic. There's Lancastrian comedian Jon Richardson (Leeds United supporter) and Yorkshire's Leigh Francis, who portrays the grating Keith Lemon. Yorkshire can also be thanked for Charlie Williams, who worked as a wartime coalminer and a post-war footballer, then became the country's first black comedian, with his catchphrase of 'me old flower' and his book called *Ee- I've Had Some Laughs*. Other classic greats include Knotty Ash's Ken Dodd, Morecambe and Wise (who proved that Lancashire and Yorkshire could get along), Ulverston's Stan Laurel of Laurel and Hardy fame, Prestwich's Victoria Wood whose *Dinner Ladies* re-runs continue to keep people laughing, and St Helens's Johnny Vegas, who I think got famous for grumbling rants in a thick Northern accent, but I can only seem to picture him in those PG Tips adverts with that monkey puppet now. Then there's Diane Morgan who played Philomena Cunk on Charlie Brooker's *Weekly Wipe* as well as *Cunk on Britain* (hilarious), and Geordie stand-up comedienne Sarah Millican, from South Shields, proving that Northern women are just as funny as the men.

Come to think of it, the funniest people I know are, in fact, people I know. The humour of your everyday Northerner is, to me, absolute gold. There's a creativity and expressiveness of language, no matter how crude or dark, and the philosophy of: if you can make a joke out of it, you should, with or without an audience of paying customers. I'll give a tiny example of how my family crack me up. When my dad turns a windy corner, he'll complain that "someone's left t' gate open" or if, when out and about, my mum suddenly stops walking he'll declare her brake lights aren't working if he runs in the back of her. This sense of humour is mentioned by W.R. Mitchell who argued in *Lancashire Mill Town Traditions* that "a cotton operative tended to laugh at himself or herself – or at life. Lancashire mill town humour was usually laconic, tongue-in-cheek, by no meaning as "cutting" as in Liverpool." Perhaps the weather has something to do with it, as we have to keep ourselves amused somehow since we can't just lounge about in a sunny plaza all day like in Spain or Italy. Either way, Northern humour is something I miss the most when I'm away. Manc poet Susan Sollazzi argued that instead of "lowering skies" oppressing us, we combat the endless cold and damp with "dark, acerbic humour." Speaking of bad weather, the topic definitely came up in conversation when I talked to Southerners about their stereotypes, though, as the author of the above poem expresses: "We, the northerners, love to complain with a smile on our faces. And I'd add to that, woe betide anyone who mocks our varied ways of speaking, too. There's no need fer that carry on.

VI. Gran's Scran

Imagine you're at a dinner party with people from around the world. Drop Italian food into the conversation and watch people salivate. Mexican? Sounds great. Sushi? Don't mind if I do. Mention British food and you'll received a confused look as your acquaintances struggle to conjure anything to mind, or be met by outright derision for suggesting we might have anything worth eating besides fish and chips.

While I understand that meat and two veg doesn't inspire sonnets, the UK does have a culinary heritage that we often know little about as we're too busy eating other people's food. Cornish pasties are basically an *empanada*, Scottish chefs are bringing back seaweed to the menu, and our bland food goes perfectly with our bland weather: we need hearty, comforting, stodge to keep us warm and happy. Northern food is no exception and has a history linked to making do with what you've got; figuring out how to feed sizable families with limited pennies and what the ground beneath your feet would let you grow. Throw into the mix some Northern generosity and you've got a recipe for a range of simple but hearty fodder.

Growing up, my sister ate banana sandwiches daily, while I lived off pilchards on toast. "They're good for yer," was my mum's trope. Pilchards are a type of sardine and the earliest recipe for pilchards on toast I could find was dated 1914 from Cheshire in *The British Home Cookery Book* by Mary Byron. Despite the banana's tropical origins, I tried to decipher if putting them in sandwiches was a Northern refinement or not. I concluded they were more of a general working-class proclivity after I learned people from Newcastle to Watford grew up eating them. Apparently during the Second World War, children used to get a banana butty alternative in the form of sugared parsnip, so much was their attachment to the delights. Such wars have, in fact, been blamed for reducing our cooking from pleasure to survival. Yet even before this, poor Lancastrian families were used to informal rationing, having had to live off jam and bread on lean days, or bread and margarine if pay day hadn't come round yet. Tinned salmon was kept for the arrival of 'comp'ny' for tea – a tradition my great aunt continued as she used to crack out the salmon finger butties when we visited. And we can't forget Orwell's disparaging description of once popular tripe, the cheap but nourishing lining of an animal's stomach. Instead, Aisling McCrea argued in an *Outline* article, 'Why British Food is Terrible', that many countries have gone through economic struggles and can still make decent grub, pointing to the UK's wider repression of sexual pleasure as to why we don't pour as much passion into our cooking. Though I think Nigella Lawson might have something to say about that.

If we start and end here, Northern food doesn't sound so appealing, and whilst it may not be the centrepiece of many Michelin star restaurants, there's more to it than meets the eye. Wiltshire-born chef Tom Kerridge described Northern food as warm, hearty and welcoming. For me, it reminds me of my grandma. I used to love running into her bungalow and being hit by a distinct combination of food smells that made up their home. The fresh bread she made weekly, sweet jam for the inside of our favourite chocolate cake, and cooked onions from whatever dinner she had on the stove. As a new vegetarian in the early noughties, to my dismay, I learned that what made a lot of her food good was that it was liberally cooked in the runoff meat juices of whatever animal had appeared in last night's meal. Those mushy peas just didn't taste the same without the bacon grease and her tomato soup had a suspicious amount of chicken bits floating in it, no matter how much she tried to convince me otherwise.

She made everything from scratch, so there was always home-baked sweets to have for 'afters'. The ritual went as follows: "What d' you want to finish off with? We've got apple pie and cream, custard tart–" to which you'd interject and appreciatively settle on custard tart but she would continue, "...and there's some courting cake left over from th' afternoon, or I've got fruit if you want it wi' a bit o' ice cream–", custard tart is fine, you'd insist, but she'd continue racking her brain and cupboards until she'd listed everything she might possibly tempt you with (there's a reason that side of the family aren't skinny). Despite all the options, my favourite of hers was her courting cake. Reference Greater Manchester's Eccles cake and nodding looks abound; mention this cake outside of Lancashire and you will likely be met with a questioning look. My grandma made a much simpler version of the fancy representations I've seen online, which was traditionally made by young ladies to show off their cooking skills to their betrothed. While in other countries, men have had to pay in livestock for their brides, apparently, we had to bake cakes to prove we were worth taking. Less privileged young Lancashire couples would court by walking to the fish and chip shop or the man who sold pies and peas then, if all was well, get married in their lunch break and returned to work in the mills until they closed at five thirty. My own grandma's cooking was also influenced by scarcity, having grown up working-class during war rationing and then, later, being a single mother with two growing children to feed.

Grandma Grime's Lancashire Courting Cake recipe

Ingredients:
½ lb margarine
1 lb flour
½ lb sugar
2 eggs
½ tsp carbonate of soda
Strawberry or raspberry jam

Directions:
Rub together the margarine, flour, baking soda, and sugar until it resembles breadcrumbs. Mix in eggs until combined.

Roll out half of the mix, spread the jam in a layer on top and place in a large greased and lined baking tray (or two smaller ones). Roll out the other half and place on top.

Brush the top with milk and bake in the oven at 375 degrees F for about 25 mins until cooked.

Use the baking paper edges to lift from the tray, remove paper, and leave to cool on a wire rack. Cut into finger-like rectangular slices and serve.

Food native to Lancashire includes wildfowl, hazelnuts, berries, and seafood such as crabs, mussels and cockles, shrimp, and sea fish. I remember going to fruit farms to do the 'pick your own' berries with my grandma (or "blegging," as they say in Yorkshire). I'd scamper down the leafy isles that towered over, putting one in the basket, one in my face (which was also my tried and tested technique for feeding ducks). I found out in adulthood that there was a fruit picking farm in the next village over from where I grew up; a well-kept secret by my hay fever-afflicted mother, else I'd have insisted she take us there every picking season. Around 5000 BC, people in Cheshire hunted red deer, wild boar, trout, and wildfowl to eat – plus wild ox and wolves back then – though forests were cleared to plant crops, animals were domesticated, and now Cheshire is largely a salt and dairy county. Lancashire on the other hand is full of small farms, with Sylvia Corbridge claiming in the 1950s, "the Lancashire man is a countryman.

My mum with grandmas and aunties in Rossendale

My maternal grandma with her friend in the valley

My maternal grandma in her hair salon in Loveclough

My mum and her friend, Sue, on holiday in Cumbria

My parents on their wedding day in Haslingdon

Outside the registry office with their parents

Me and my sister at home in Chester

Eating my grandma's scones in Over Kellet

He is a farmer at heart, living in a county which has more small farms than any other. It has long been his custom to own his bit of land and set a cow, a pig and a few hens on it. When this is not possible, he wrests a plot of land from his local council, builds himself a shed, and spends his retirement growing vegetables and "a few chrysants for the missus"."

My mum grew up on a smallholding where she tells me she would ride their cow – couldn't afford a horse – and my grandma had a greenhouse well into her eighties, in which she grew tomatoes and beans. My sister and I grew up with apple trees and a rhubarb patch and a mum who made the fruit into delicious pies and crumbles (the trees weren't bad for climbing either). I was dubbed green fingered ever since I grew peas in winter in dad's shed when I was eleven – or, as they'd say in Lancashire, I can "mek nowt grow summat" – and have always loved knowing where my food comes from.

As well as my green fingers, I also inherited my cooking abilities from my maternal lineage. When the country was ordered into lockdown at the height of the pandemic, I figured then was as good a time as any to experiment with cooking some Northern food I hadn't got round to making yet. As a veggie, I didn't go near Bury's black pudding (there is a Black Pudding Throwing Championship in the town, where you can apparently pay two quid to lob 'em at Yorkshire puddings to see how many you can knock down. Friendly competition, with a slight dig at the Tykes). I also avoided Teesside's chicken parmo, Cumberland sausage, or an oddly named catfish with a face like the back end of a beaten-up bus called the Scarborough Woof. I did, however, set my sights on making any animal-free Northern food that had so far escaped my kitchen. I'm ashamed to say I'd never previously made a Lancashire hotpot, having only lived off the frozen ones from Iceland as a newly vegetarian teenager. My own Lancastrian grandma and mother were more partial to making a corned beef hash than a hotpot, popular after the Second World War due to the use of tinned meat during rationing. The hotpot also had humble beginnings as a convenience meal for the working-class population of the pre-industrialised North as many women worked from home spinning cotton. As Lancashire industrialised, the hotpot could be left stewing for hours, thus retaining its popularity as the family went off to work in the factories. I finally got around to making my own vegan version and I caught my mum, who insisted she didn't want some if it didn't have meat in, sneaking a taste when she thought I wasn't looking.

After the humble hotpot I made butter pie, another Lancashire favourite, filling it with buttery potatoes and not much else. As I was lulled into a rhythm rolling out the pastry onto a flour-covered kitchen top, I thought of all my ancestors who'd spent hours in the kitchen, baking bread and rolling out pie crusts to feed the family... of all the housewives who entered paid work during the First World War in the flour mills in Cheshire or the army biscuit factories in Lancashire to feed the country. Lowering the bottom into its metal casing, I worried my pie would come out bland or dry, but it was delicious and, accompanied by liberal amounts of onion gravy, went down a treat. Butter pie is also called Friday pie as it was eaten by Catholics on the day they abstained from eating meat, particularly in Preston (formerly known as Priest Town) which in the nineteenth century took in many Irish immigrants. Said pie also gets an honorary mention in the Paul McCartney song 'Uncle Albert/Admiral Halsey'.

Another deserving mention was invented in 2012 for the four hundredth anniversary of the Pendle Witch Trials, named the Malkin Pie after the tower in which the older witch, Demdike, was said to live. The pie is a five-layered meat-fest of lamb, beef, and bacon, with some leek and carrots stuffed in between, and can be found at some Lancashire farmers' markets or sold on the day of a solstice in honour of the women. I have never come across this pie myself (and haven't the foggiest if anyone's attempted to make a vegetarian version), though apparently you can source it from its creators at Sanwitches of Sabden. Notice a theme?

Speaking of pies (which we have to when talking about Northern food), I'm told Wigan is the "land of the pie-eaters". Whilst this sounded to me like they were the unbeaten champions of a pie-eating contest – they do love a pie barm – it is supposedly a name gained from the General Strike of 1926 in which starving workers returned to their jobs, thus having to eat 'humble pie'. Either way, Wiganers have leaned into it, and you can now order tiered wedding pies instead of the traditional cakes. But if you're just after a regular pie, well, Northerners will tell you that pies are best eaten with a load of gravy on 'em. A friend of mine, while living in London, was 'outed' as a Northerner when she kept asking the waiter for more gravy for her Sunday roast. "They literally gave me, like, a thimble," she complained in earnest. You can't have a dry Yorkshire pud, and we like to have to fish our veg out of that delicious gravy pool. Or, as Terry Wogan commented upon trying a pudding on *Terry and Mason's Great Food Trip*, we serve our gravy "thick enough to trot a mouse across." I also saw an episode of ITV's *Inside Britain's Food Factories*, when they were in Hull at a Yorkshire pudding factory and one of the managers declared, "I don't have blood that runs through my veins, I have batter," so true was her love for the floury baskets. Controversially, my mum and sister were partial to eating Yorkshire puds with sugar as a dessert as kids. Either I didn't like to, or I've blocked it from my memory.

As is illustrated by our pies and puds, us Northerners don't need food to be fancy to appreciate it. We are known for our love of Greggs (I'm more of a Sayers gal, personally) and every time I return to the UK, I made a beeline for the nearest veggie sausage roll. We are partial to a 'beige buffet': a sea of pastry and bread-based products with a cursory bit of lettuce and dried up cucumber crowned as the 'salad'. I remember having a vegetarian buffet for my eighteenth birthday and I caught my grandma with her head in the fridge consuming her own contraband: "can't have a buffet without pork pies".

Once I'd had a good crack at all the carbs, I proceeded to make a Northeastern favourite, Pease Pudding, a sort of yellow split pea mush. OK, so that's not the most flattering description, but don't be put off if you like mushy peas or hummus. I found a back-up tin of readymade stuff just in case my culinary adventure ended badly, but it turned out lovely scooped up with fresh-from-the-oven bread. I then had the following refrain stuck in my head for the rest of the day:

Pease pudding hot
Pease pudding cold
Pease pudding in the pot
nine days old.

Sticking with pulses, Parched Peas were a treat traditionally served on bonfire night with vinegar. The mention of them even made my unsentimental dad nostalgic: "Eeh, it's been a while since I 'ad black peas," he declared, his eyes reaching back across time. It was a mission to track any black peas down to make it, though I found some at an eco-store and paid twice as much as they cost for delivery in order to transport him back to his childhood. Unfortunately, while cooking the peas, I got distracted listening to a podcast advert about how men need to put respect before romance when it comes to relationships, resulting in my peas becoming extra parched. I told myself the smoked taste was an added twist of authenticity, not unlike the aroma of a bonfire, doused them in vinegar and ate them with chips. Ever one to bring me down a peg, my dad turned his nose up at them, claiming it wasn't the same if you hadn't just bought them off the street.

One of my mum's childhood favourites, on the other hand, was potted shrimps. She displayed childlike excitement when we went to Morecambe Bay specifically so she could get a pot after she'd ordered some in a gastropub the night before on a trip to the Lakes but screwed her face up, complaining that "this isn't what they're supposed to be like." It was, it turns out, supposed look like a gaggle of tiny sea maggots drowning in butter in a Styrofoam cup. So that is what we found her on the prom as I was dragged away from the coin push machines.

I was not in a rush to recreate anything eel-related. As a teen, my dad would get the six am train from Preston to Arnside to fish for them with his mates, taking them home for my grandma to fry in butter. My mum recently unearthed an old edition of *The Lancashire Cook Book* from the Lancashire Federation of Women's Institute in the depths of one of those drawers where odd takeaway leaflets get shoved. The cookbook lists eel pie under 'Old Traditional Recipes', along with Bury simnel cake and fair cakes from Garstang and Slaidburn. Also in the booklet was a section called 'Posh Nosh for Children's Parties' that included hobgoblin soup (which, disappointingly, seemed to be carrot soup with an exciting name to trick children into eating it) and a "yum yum" cake made with walnuts and cherries.

In addition to the love of a good pie, many Northerners

have a sweet tooth. My maternal grandma's handbag was well-stocked with Kendal Mint Cake, a peppermint-flavoured confectionary made in that Cumbrian town. The little packets would rustle every time she reached in to retrieve her purse or keys and, like a Pavlovian pup, I'd lift my face expectantly at the sound, hoping to receive a piece. When we'd visit my paternal grandparents in Preston, my sister and I would sit on the floor up against the fireplace, eagerly awaiting the gingerbread men we knew our grandma had bought from the bakery down the road; each time as exciting as the last when we bit into an arm or a leg. According to the Lake District's renowned Grasmere gingerbread makers, the biscuits were originally given by knights as love tokens, though in a much more decorative state than the ones we see today.

Though I love cooking, baking is a very hit and miss affair with me. I believe cooking is an art, baking a science, and I'm much better at being creative than precise. Accordingly, I enlisted my brother-in-law, a former chef, to make our own city's dessert: Chester pudding. None of us had had heard of it, as it long ago went out of fashion, so I figured it time to bring it back. The pudding is a Victorian precursor to lemon meringue, cooked in a shallow dish and with the addition of crushed almonds it's flipping delicious. And that's coming from someone who is not a dessert person. Chef Nigella Lawson described it as "heavenly" when she visited the city. If that's not a seal of approval, I don't know what is.

Across the Pennines you can find Whitby Buns, a lemon iced bread bun, and a favourite of mine from my high school cafeteria which often provided my sustenance for the day since vegetarian options were direly lacking. Then there's Pontefract Cake, a coin-like disc of the town's trademark liquorice which monks used to grow for medicinal purposes after it was imported from the Middle East by crusaders; as well as Everton toffees from which the football team gets their name. The nation's favourites to gorge on at Christmas time, Quality Street chocolates, come from Halifax, and Terry's and Roundtree originated in York in the mid-nineteenth century by Quaker families pushing chocolate as an alcohol alternative. West Yorkshire is also home to the so-called Rhubarb Triangle – nine square miles of the fruit (though it used to cover thirty square miles before the Second World War) – which is native to Siberia but a lover of the county's cold, wet winters. Back on the coast, both Blackpool and Scarborough make colourful rock candy sticks for sticky-fingered children to break their teeth on. Or rot them with its pure sugar if they survive the crunch, though I'm told there are sugar-free varieties available now, including rock dummies for babies.

On top of pies and puddings, most Northerners also love a good chippy tea. So much so that music group Lancashire Hotpots have a song called 'Chippy Tea' with the lyrics, "you keep givin' posh nosh... but I'm a working man from Lancashire/And I wants a chippy tea." *Gogglebox*'s Malone family from Manchester argued in one episode over whether hummus was posh, with the dad coming down firmly on the affirmative side, as he reminisced about how he grew up eating chip butties and even bread butties (you read right, it's a slice of bread in between two other slices of bread).

My mum recalls how on Friday nights the entire town of Rawtenstall would be down the chippy, though her mum had to make their own fish 'n' chips as they couldn't afford the luxury. If you live in London nowadays, you might also struggle, as the *Yorkshire Post* reported in 2021, that a Tyke dad was seeking therapy after being charged £54 for a chippy tea for his family when visiting the capital. One solution is to befriend those who can get you mates' rates. My childhood friend's grandparents used to run a chippy in Chorley, and a work mate of mine from Greater Manchester tells me she grew up a designated mushy pea taster for her parents at their chippy after coming over from Hong Kong. As a vegetarian, 'going the chippy' is still an essential when-at-the-seaside tradition for me. Back when I lived in Leeds in 2014, there was a hole-in-the-wall shop near the Corn Exchange that a friend and I frequented for pea fritters. Covered in salt and vinegar, they were delicious. I haven't found them anywhere else since and the place is long closed. I have, however, figured out how to make the fritters and even recently discovered a recipe for crafting them out of leftover chips that have also gone mushy and would otherwise end up in the bin or the dog's slobbering face. I can highly recommend. Another favourite of mine – chips, cheese, and gravy – is a distinctly Northern delight. Though it's mocked by Southerners, it's basically Canadian poutine without the fancy-sounding French name. And probably a lot more oil. I'm also partial to chips and curry sauce. Either of those with a side of mushy peas. And scraps (batter that's left after the fish frying) if they're going. And maybe some bread to make a chip butty.

Of course, chippy tea doesn't involve dunking your chips in a hot cup of chai. 'Tea' is what we Northerners call dinner, 'dinner' is what we call lunch, and many of us call a cuppa a 'brew'. 'Supper' is jam butties with a glass of milk before bed, not what posh people call their evening meal. Confused? We at least all agree that breakfast is breakfast. I grew up shouting into the kitchen: "What's for tea?" followed by asking what was "for afters", promptly adapting to calling it "dinner" and "dessert" to avoid complications abroad. As for a good brew, my friend and I – typical teenagers – longed for things we couldn't have, in our case, a tea tap that endlessly poured out a perfect temperature cuppa to right all wrongs in the world for a minute or so. (Apparently Persians had this idea a long time ago, inventing a giant pot called a Samovar to hold tea with a convenient tap to refill when your glass runs empty.) As is so well expressed by Wigan-born poet Lemn Sissay:

I'm a lifted kettle me
I rise and I shine
One cup of tea
And the world's mine

Sylvia Corbridge wrote: "If I must paint the Lancashire woman then let it be the portrait of a friend with an extended hand, work-worn through centuries of labour, grasping a well-sugared cup of tea." When I moved back to Leeds in 2022, I popped to my local to grab some tea and the smallest I could find was a 210-bag box of Yorkshire Tea, which was fine by me. That said, I am partial to Earl Grey after a friend's London-born mum got me hooked on it. She was the kind of mum who brought us cups of tea on a tray and didn't mind when we polished off all the brownies from the fridge. The story goes that, in the nineteenth century, the Earl of Northumberland rescued a Chinese man from drowning who then gave him the recipe in thanks for his life. The result is black tea infused with bergamot oil which is a bit posher than a builder's brew. Our other mate who also got lured in by the delicate aroma to this day asks if I want "earl gay", as if that makes it less posh and therefore okay to drink. Amusingly, the LBGTQIA+ community created an actual Earl Gay tea made of Earl Grey, spice mix and 'pride' to celebrate "the awesomeness of gayness". I, of course, immediately ordered some.

Another quintessentially Northern fluid is the popular soft drink, Vimto, created in Manchester in 1908 by a Blackburn man who was a wholesale herbalist, though its production has since travelled across the Pennines to Yorkshire. It was created to offer "vim and vigour" though Jennings argued that it "tastes like seven packets of blackcurrant jelly dissolved in Perrier water", which seems a fair description. Interestingly, far from the Northwest, Vimto has a significant market in the

Gulf States during Ramadan where it frequents the table after daily fasting, with one Dubai engineer going as far as to say that "Ramadan is not Ramadan without Vimto."[15]

As well as soft drinks, the North has a history with those of the harder variety. At one point in time, drinking beer was safer than drinking water as the fermentation process killed some of the harmful bacteria that could make people sick. What's more, public houses were places where workers could meet at the weekend and celebrate not going to work the next day. While today we have safe tap water in abundance, the latter tradition remains. Where there is a North/South divide is price, as a pint in London can cost more than twice of one in Newcastle. The North also produces a fair amount of decent beer. As well as laying claim to having the most Michelin-starred restaurants anywhere outside of London, Yorkshire has more breweries than any county in England. They've even nicked the distinctive working man's beer, Newcastle Brown Ale, which is now produced in Tadcaster. Tetley's brewery was founded in 1822 in Leeds, producing the popular Tetley's Ale (the second highest selling in the world after John Smiths) until 2012, when production also moved to Tadcaster and Hartlepool. Not all Northerners liked the habit of stopping by the pub on the way home from work, though, as the temperance movement began in Preston in the 1800s with people intercepting workers at the end of their day and issuing warnings such as "lips that touch liquor shall never touch mine." It didn't last long, mind, and the last known original temperance bar in England can be found in my mum's borough of Rawtenstall.

In 2016 documentary, *The Hairy Bikers' Pubs that Built Britain*, the enthusiastic hairy Lancashire-County Durham duo travelled around to find the stories of our nation's boozers. Starting in Yorkshire, then moving to the Lakes and down to Manchester and Liverpool, they ended their tour in

Carlisle where they discovered a government scheme aimed at improving the First World War effort by taking over all the pubs and breweries near the biggest munitions works in Gretna Green. Apparently, there used to be so many pubs in Carlilse you could swing from door to door, so I'm guessing the government had their work cut out.

If said Hairy Bikers had zipped over to Northern Europe they would have found a stew-like dish called lobskaus, or skaus for short (sound familiar?). Turns out you needn't go so far though, as you can get the dish in Liverpool. My sister stumbled across the meal whilst in Hamburg and returned to me with this tale: it turns out that Liverpool, being a seaport, heartily adopted the dish that was popular with sailors and then, in some unknown leap of historical logic, Liverpudlians became thereafter known as Scousers. What a fusion of three of my favourite things: travel, language, and food. Apparently, there's also a veggie version called 'blind scouse', so I'm adding that to my list as I've yet to come across it.

Speaking of meat-free fare, the Vegetarian Society's first public meeting was in Manchester in 1848 and it currently holds its headquarters in Altrincham. Key members of the Society were from the Bible Christian Church founded in Salford who viewed a meat-free diet as an act of temperance. Despite such Northern beginnings, when I became vegetarian in Chester twenty-something years ago, I would end up trawling from restaurant to restaurant looking for food I could eat. Fast-forward to the present and there are many vegan cafés and food outlets, so I often get overwhelmed as there are more than two veggie choices on a menu.

Despite being a long-time vegetarian, cheese is the bane of my wannabe vegan life. Eggs? I have scrambled tofu. Milk? Coconut beats dairy in a coffee anyway. But cheese is hard to replace. The closest I've found is a nut-based alternative from Soul Cheeze, a one-woman business in Cheshire's former county town, Nantwich (I recommend the smoked one). In the name of investigative journalism, I took it upon myself to gorge on a selection of Northern cheeses starting with one immortalised by Wallace and Gromit – Wensleydale. Said cheese is often enjoyed with fruit cake so I, of course, went on a hunt for the combo and found it in a community café in Leeds, its lactic bite complementing a rich curranty sweetness.

Two other dales provide us with cheesey goodness: Dovedale from the Peak District and Swaledale from North Yorkshire, though I am yet to have the pleasure of sampling them. Kirkham Farmhouse Lancashire – chosen because I have family in Kirkham, though it was named after the maker, Mrs Kirkham, who resides in countryside north of Preston – is a crumblier cheese that I ate with local chutney. I finished off with Cheshire – believed to be Britain's oldest recorded cheese as it was mentioned in the eleventh century Domesday Book – whacked on a slice of toast. Speaking of toast, my maternal great-grandfather had two great pieces of advice. The first: when buttering toast "take care of the edges and the middle takes care of itself", counsel I have heeded throughout my life; dry crusts are the worst. The second was, plainly put: "If it's brown, it's done. If it's black, it's buggered."

While living in Leeds I co-founded a Vegetarian Food Society at university (2009 winner of Best New Society, thank you very much) for vegetarians and meat-eaters alike to explore the joys of "food without a face". We'd do occasional trips to Kirkgate Market which is where I was introduced to the joy of harissa on hummus pitta and learned that Marks & Spencer began as a humble stall here in 1884, destined to become responsible for mildly pornographic posh nosh ads.

We also can't talk about British food in general, and Northern food in particular, without noting the effect that immigration has had on our gastronomic habits. Northern food culture – like any kind of culture – is not a static noun but a living practice, and new arrivals co-exist alongside the older traditions. Some fusions became solid additions to our palette, such as the humble chip shop curry sauce. What's more, fried fish was thought to have come to our shores via Spanish and Portuguese Jewish refugees during the sixteenth century. Plus, it was a Jewish Eastern European refugee who reportedly opened the first fish and chip shop in London around 1860 (though some argue the humble chippy already existed up North, but no-one cared to document that until one popped up in the capital). Following this, our nation's unofficial national dish is, of course, curry. The first British recipe, published in 1747, was for a pilau meal and such is our love that we have a National Curry Week every October.

To cater to British tastes, the Pearl of India restaurant in Yorkshire offers curried Yorkshire puddings and there exist recipes for onion bhaji pud. The traditionalists, however, can be spoilt for choice at Manchester's Curry Mile in Rusholme. That's right, a whole mile rammed with the culinary delights of South Asia. The creamy, orange-coloured Chicken Tikka Masala was apparently created in the UK, legend has it that it was created for the British tastebuds who wanted their meat served in gravy but couldn't handle anything too spicy. After living abroad seriously upped my tolerance for heat, I once asked for a spicier side sauce in the Lakes after the 'spicy' dish I'd ordered was giving me zero tongue tingle. "Careful," my acquaintance warned. "Our Lee did that once and it was taken as a challenge. What they brought blew his socks off."

Bradford is by legend the place to go for a good curry – it ought to be on everyone's 'to visit' list, especially since being awarded UK City of Culture for 2025 – though its neighbour Leeds boasts a few decent curry houses of its own. One was a converted public toilet in Hyde Park – top marks for novelty – but my favourite was a little place called Nazam's in Woodhouse. With a shabby living room vibe, BYOB, friendly staff, and naan as big as your head, it won over my heart and hungry belly. (FYI, saying 'naan bread' translates to 'bread bread', in the same way that 'chai tea' makes 'tea tea'.)

Wherever you end up in the UK, "going for an Indian" or "ordering a Chinese" are now staple activities. Historian Panikos Panayi argued in *Spicing Up Britain* that immigration liberated our palates after a post-war diet slump of meat and two veg. That said, I still think traditional British food is worth sticking up for, we just need to invest as much love and effort into it as other nation's do their foods.

Food writer Josh Barrie wrote that pride, practicality and hospitality make regional food what it is up North and I agree. Food is not only sustenance but tradition rooted in history and place, as well as a documentation of culture reaffirming and reinventing itself. It is nostalgia and comfort; a way to make new memories with loved ones or renew community bonds. It's the dishes that are never as good in the restaurant as they are when your mum makes them, or the biscuits that only taste right when they have the faint odour of your grandparents' house clinging to their crummy edges. It's the roasties that you wait all year for as no-one makes them as good as your brother-in-law does at Christmas, or the bakery that reminds you of your gran. It's teaching the next generation of the family how to make pastry as their tiny hands get covered in flour and butter and they impatiently wait for the pie to come out the oven. It's the curry house with the '70s carpet, or the greasy chippy of your youth that you used to stop in on your way home from a night out to soak up all the sugary alcopops you'd consumed while tearing up the dancefloor. And it is, of course, knowing that gravy is not to be used sparingly and that it's best not to start the great bun/barm/bap/bin lid/breadcake debate unless you want to a fight. Which you might get if you've had one too many and are freezing your arse off in a midnight queue for the chippy.

VII. A Northerner By Any Other Name

Writer Anita Sethi told the story of how Prince Charles asked her where she was from, and when she replied "Manchester", he commented that she didn't look like she was from there. This doesn't inspire much confidence in our now King, as he should really know that Manchester is one of the country's multicultural hubs. And, for anyone who needs reminding – and as the title of Anita's book *I Belong Here* would suggest – people who aren't white can also come from Manchester/England/Europe (delete as appropriate). As much as it might feel like migration is a newish phenomenon to certain parts of the UK, the North has been shaped by immigration from the Romans to the Vikings, and there were also people from Africa living in a Roman Fort in Cumbria as far back as the third century AD. However, taking as a starting point the more recent and well-known history of immigration, this chapter discusses the struggles and contributions of those who have found their way to the North to make it their home, discussing topics from rotis and riots to colonisation and collaboration.

Aside from the fact that our monarchy has long consisted of marrying nobility from other countries, even if you're not royal, London is by far the most popular destination for migrants, particularly non-EU immigrants. The city is known around the world for being a multicultural and multiracial city with 60 per cent of the population comprising people of colour and around one million identifying as mixed-race. The latter category is the UK's fastest growing demographic, though not a new occurrence and certainly not just limited to London. From as early as the 1920s it was not uncommon to see interracial relationships in places like South Shields and Toxteth, Liverpool. Cities like London or Birmingham are commonly associated with immigration, but it has also shaped those in the North such as Manchester, Leeds, and Bradford, as well as in smaller towns like Blackburn (almost a third of the population identify as Indian or Pakistani), Hull (with many Iraqis) or Warrington (popular with Slovakians).

While London's West Indian community brought us the Notting Hill Carnival in 1966 – attended by millions, it's the biggest street carnival in Europe – Chapeltown's West Indian community in Leeds launched their own in 1967, hundreds of thousands of revellers attending every year. Manchester's Moss Side, home to many Afro-Caribbeans and Indians who moved there after the Second World War, made the place a thriving cultural centre for immigrants with a strong working-class community identity and Manchester's Carnival was started by the Caribbean community there in 1972.

Of the half a million people in Manchester, 66 per cent identify as white British, 17 per cent Asian, 8.5 per cent black, 5 per cent mixed-race, 2 per cent Arab, and 1 per cent weren't offered a box to tick that suited them, so they got stuck with the vaguely ominous label of 'Other'. There are nearly 200 languages spoken in the city and the university draws a fair few international students as well. Manchester has the largest

Jewish community outside of London after European Jews fled in the eighteenth and nineteenth centuries. The Industrial Revolution also saw an influx of Irish immigrants looking for job opportunities and, after the Second World War, many South Asians, Caribbeans and East Africans found a home in the city. Manchester is also home to the third largest Chinese community in Europe. Chinatown emerged in the 1970s, announcing its presence with a giant arch – a gift directly from China and a necessary arrow pointing to the area as you might walk past it unawares otherwise. The gateway is perhaps the most exciting visual there, unless you go during Chinese New Year, when visitors are greeted with lion and dragon dances. It was also the largest Chinatown archway until, in typical rivalry, Liverpool decided it didn't want to be outdone in 2000 when it got a bigger one. But to move on from a superficial "tepees and tacos" multi-culturalism, let's dig a little deeper into what it took to get us to where we are now. Because, as well as expanding our culinary repertoire, immigration has asked us to decide what kind of nation we are, pushing us to put our money where our mouth is. It has challenged and enriched our society, bringing us (whether some liked it or not) face-to-face with citizens from the empire the Brits had created when a domino effect of independence movements occurred across Asia and then Africa after the Second World War.

When World War II was still raging on, Britain – or at least one tiny Lancashire village – showed itself to be welcoming to newcomers. In June 1943, soldiers from the American 1511th Regiment went for a drink at Ye Old Hob Inn, a quaint thatched roof pub in Bamber Bridge, three miles south of Preston. The US Armed Forces were racially segregated at the time and the story goes that they demanded a bar where black people could go to drink away from white soldiers. The village pubs defied this call and supported the troops, with barmaid Gillian Vesey making the white soldiers wait their turn to be served rather than expecting to get their drinks before black colleagues. The local women wanted to learn the popular Jitterbug dance and apparently that rankled, causing one lieutenant to comment: "One thing I noticed here and which I don't like is the fact that the English don't draw any colour line. The English must be pretty ignorant. I can't see how a white girl could associate with a negro." A white officer confronted the black soldiers drinking with the townspeople and tried to arrest Private Eugene Nunn for not wearing proper uniform. A white British soldier reportedly asked: "Why do you want to arrest them? They're not doing anything or bothering anybody?" The military police were sent for, the soldiers raided the arms stock in the meantime, and all hell broke loose with one soldier killed and various people on both sides injured. A court martial convicted thirty-two soldiers of mutiny, but blamed poor leadership and racism within the military police.

Despite the anti-racist attitudes of the Bamber Bridgers in this story, only three miles north in Preston my dad recalls signs in B&B windows saying "No Irish, No Blacks, No dogs" in the 1950s and early '60s. I don't know if the clientele at Ye Old Hob Inn were not representative of the majority of the populace at the time, if Preston was just less tolerant of change – England having been overwhelmingly white before the war – or if opinions had soured in the ten years or so after this story that it took for my dad to be born and learn to read. My mum said there were never any signs like that in her village of Crawshawbooth, though my dad teased "that's cos you lived in t' sticks and no one wanted to move there." My mum quickly protested that there was a German woman who lived on their street, before adding: "though folks were wary of her presence", the war a lingering memory in the collective consciousness. Writer Grace Dent wrote of a similar lack of diversity in Cumbria when she was growing up there in the 1980s and '90s, saying that people of colour rarely found themselves in Carlisle, being pelted by sleet, and decided that this was where they should settle down.

When the war ended in 1945, orphaned Jewish children from across Europe were given new homes around the UK. For many, their first port of call was an empty factory-turned-reception centre at Lake Windemere, where a team of psychologists and counsellors worked with as many as three hundred orphaned children who had been liberated from concentration camps. The children stayed there for six months until they were sent out to join British society. Initially they had two-year visas but, with no family to return to, many stayed in the UK such as Sam Laskier and Ike Alterman who became businessmen in Manchester.

Despite such tales, not all people have been welcoming to newcomers and tensions between different communities led to Britain's first modern so-called 'race riot' after the end of the First World War in 1919 in South Shields, "a deeply small town stuck like a piece of punctuation at the end of economic life", according to Jennings on his visit some eighty years later. Yemeni sailors after the First World War had committed that age-old offence of "taking our jobs". Street violence broke out, with whites attacking Arab boarding houses and cafés. Some of these tensions are detailed in local author Catherine Cookson's novel, *Colour Blind*, and, if the story is anything to go by, racism was alive and well in the Northeast around this time. The riots did not begin and end in South Shields, however. Liverpool also saw them in their 'sailor town' – a part of the city populated by Chinese, West African and Caribbean, Scandinavian, Russian, Ukrainian and Italian seafaring men. While such men were welcomed during the First World War to fill the wartime labour shortage in the UK, when the English men returned from war, there was the problem of too many people and not enough jobs. After a black man was stabbed by two Scandinavian men for refusing to share his cigarettes, other men retaliated, attacking a Scandinavian pub. Riots broke out resulting in the death of a black man called Charles Wotten who was chased off the docks, and the police put repatriation efforts into place. Unrest spread across not just the North but the rest of the country with riots in Salford, Hull, Glasgow, London, Newport, and Cardiff.

Sadly, clashes didn't stop there. The year 1930 saw another riot in South Shields over scarcity of work and a slew of deportations followed. Then, when many immigrants arrived after the Second World War, initially thriving areas were hit hard when poverty rose in the '70s across the North as old industries disappeared and jobs moved to London, as well as the slum clearances which saw many houses demolished, breaking up communities. Riots occurred in 1981 between Moss Side residents and the police, as well as in Toxteth in Liverpool and Brixton in London. Merseyside in 1981 was the worst hit by the recession with high levels of unemployment and Toxteth the most badly affected. The Toxteth riots were triggered by the Merseyside police, who had a reputation for racist policing, heavy-handling a man during an arrest whilst an angry crowd watched on. A tactic for dispersing people, picked up from Northern Ireland, was driving cars at high speed into the crowd and, in this instance, a disabled man called David Moore was killed when he was hit by a Land Rover. Two officers were charged with manslaughter but cleared the next year.

That said, justice does not always deem some above the law. I was recently showing two US-based friends around Leeds when we came across a blue plaque on a bridge over the river. It informed us that a man named David Oluwale, who had come to Leeds from Nigeria in 1949, had been "hounded to his death" in 1969 by police who, in an unusual turn of events, did get convicted. As we were sombrely taking in this information, a kid approached us with a gaggle of his mates hovering behind him asking if he could take a picture of us next to the commemoration for a school project of plaques around the city. After clarifying he wasn't going to anything weird with it, we turned to pose and he gave a 'thumbs up'. As a reflex, so did we, so now if they zoom in on the text, we could be construed as three white people offering a horrifically inappropriate reaction to the material, and his class presentation could take a whole other direction.

But maybe I'm going about this the wrong way. Rather than starting with who came here when and what happened, we should start with where people arrived from and why. In the 2021 England and Wales Census, Asian ethnic groups made up the largest population at 9.6 per cent (around five and a half million) after white Brits at 74.4 per cent. Ambalavaner Sivanandan, the Sri Lankan born director of the Institute of Race Relations (1973-2013), famously and succinctly stated: "We are here because you were there."

Britain's colonial ties to Asia mean that immigration from the continent should not be surprising. During the Anglo-Sikh wars of the nineteenth century, many Sikh Punjabis were recruited to fight for Queen and country; then in the twentieth century, over one million Indians fought in the First World War with the (unfulfilled) promise of decolonisation. Around sixty thousand died and the same number again were injured. Further millions (yes, millions) were killed by the Spanish Flu as the disease was spread around by returning soldiers. The Brits finally agreed to leave India in 1947 after a successful independence movement led by, among others, Mahatma Gandhi. Around 25 per cent of the population were Muslim and tensions between Hindus and Muslims had been brewing for a while under colonial rule. Violence spread leaving thousands dead and many more injured. British politicians decided to fast-track the 'Partition' of India in 1947, splitting the country into Hindu India and Muslim Pakistan, or at least that was the idea. Violence ensued, as well as mass migration, as people scrambled to match their religion with their homeland, leaving hundreds of thousands dead and millions displaced. (I highly recommend the book *A Suitable Boy* by Indian author, Vikram Seth. It combines a Bollywood soap opera of characters and love affairs against the politics of post-Partition India.)

As a result, many came to the UK fleeing violence, then again in the 1970s when East and West Pakistan had a civil war, leading to the creation of Bangladesh. Others came simply in search of economic opportunities when the UK needed workers after the war. However, in 1962 the Commonwealth Act tried to limit the influx of incomers when we decided we'd had enough help, thank you very much.

Many who did make the cut ended up, amongst other places, in Bradford due to its textile industry built on wool and migration. In 2020, Bradford civic society displayed family photos of the first waves of immigrants coming to the city in an exhibition called *4000 Miles to Home*. Yorkshire offered a much harsher and colder climate requiring clothing to be adapted, and assimilation was encouraged with rumours reportedly circulating that to be seen without socks would lead to arrest. As the women arrived to join their men, they re-established customs such as dress, food, and family traditions, and some Sikh women also joined the workforce, particularly where there were already female employees in the mills in the '50s. When the next generation of the families were born in England, however, people had to shift their mindset from being economic migrants with the idea of returning, to being British.

The 1960s brought with it a slew of anti-racism laws passed to avoid discrimination of workers and tenants, though with varying levels of success. Since Islamophobia has for a while been Britain's racist flavour of the week, Bradford has seen its share of racial tension that boiled over into riots in 1995. These were largely ignored and swept nicely under the wool rug, but in 2001 race riots bubbled up again, lasting three days, leading the city to become known as a 'racial tinderbox', with the Asian community and the white working-class community at odds after "sleepwalking our way to segregation", according to British Guianese broadcaster Trevor Phillips. The rioting promptly spread across the Pennines to Oldham and Burnley. In response to the 2001 riots in Northern English cities, New Labour assumed that the problem was a lack of assimilation, though others argued that the problem was second-generation immigrants expected economic and legal equality but instead experienced racism and a lack of opportunities, exacerbated by the social segregation of one group of marginalised people against another.

So, why remember this history of rioting? Not to add fuel to the xenophobic fire about immigrants as violent troublemakers, but to critically understand our own story; the story of Britain and of the North. After we got rich off others' resources, we were eventually chucked out by wave after wave of freedom movements, we then had to invite citizens of these newly independent states to our lands to help us with that pesky economy which, like a beast raised from the underworld, still demanded its sacrifices. Upon arriving and facing racism and inequality, some were understandably a bit peeved. Whilst the recent disaster that was the Brexit campaign reminded us that, in times of austerity, immigrants are often scapegoated, history patiently waits to be called upon to show us this is not a new occurrence as economic scarcity hits underprivileged communities with a double whammy, through the irony of being the most likely to suffer and yet simultaneously being blamed for others' misery to add insult to injury.

In response to hostility and racism, immigrants have time and again banded in solidarity through places of worship or formal organisations such as the League of Coloured People active in the 1920s and '30s who campaigned for black nurses to be accepted at Manchester infirmary, as well as smashing stereotypes in the '70s when immigrant Asian women led industrial protests in London and Leicester, becoming known as the 'strikers in saris'. Riots are a form of protest against injustice, a sort of 'last resort' move after other avenues have been exhausted and ignored. The author of *Why I'm No Longer Talking to White People About Race*, Londoner Reni Eddo-Lodge, explains succinctly: "...the extremity of a riot only ever reflects the extremity of the living situation of said rioters." In addition, such action continues the centuries-old tradition we have here in the North of working-class people demanding their rights and, I don't know about you, but that makes me proud. Just as Moss Side's Emmeline Pankhurst and her lot weren't satisfied with voting rights for men only (and had to fight to get what they wanted since asking politely didn't work), Moss Side and other communities of colour who rioted in the twenty-first century similarly weren't satisfied with being treated like second-class citizens. Most recently, across the UK thousands of people took part in peaceful protests as part of the Black Lives Matter movement in June 2020 – even in my majority white city. One sign read: "You know it's bad when Chester marches." Another on a protester's dog read: "I'm colour-blind and even I can see the UK is racist."

Returning to Bradford, the city has the largest Pakistani community in England, as well as a number of asylum seekers including Nobel Prize-winning education advocate Malala and her family. One of the directors of the Bradford Literature Festival uses classic English lit to highlight the connection between women's lives during the Brontë era and modern-day experiences for some Pakistani girls in the area, arguing that the Yorkshire Moors continue to allow people to express themselves outside of the domestic space. Universities also play a role in ensuring that multiculturalism is celebrated. It was at the University of Leeds that I joined Student Action for Refugees where they offered conversational English to asylum seekers and refugees, promoting community between newcomers and students outside of the university 'bubble'. I also joined the United Nations Youth Association and, as you can imagine, it included Brits from different backgrounds as well as people from all over the world. These people taught me not only about their countries, but inspired me to be a better citizen both in the UK and the wider world.

There are also people working to celebrate the city's diversity and educate one another about their cultural traditions and way of life. As well as community centres and churches, Leeds has a number of temples and mosques and I remember Hyde Park's Makkah Mosque opening one day to the wider community. The outside of the building is decorated in orange, red, and blue horizontal tiles wrapping around the exterior and the inside is patterned with lines from the Quran, written in Arabic, adorning the inside of the domes. Such initiatives for cross-cultural understanding are important as the population of non-UK born inhabitants of Yorkshire and the Humber increased from 295,000 in 2005 to 479,000 in 2015, and you can't get to know your neighbour by staring at them from the other side of the road.

Where I lived back in 2010, there were tensions between white working-class families, Asian working-class families, and the students with their laptops and PlayStations which were begging to be nicked when someone left the window open on the way to the Otley Run (speaking from experience). The mostly white middle-class folks tended to live in bigger houses in the leafy suburbs outside of the city centre, and the yuppies by the river. Maconie argued, after being called a "rich bastard" by some teenagers for using a taxi in Leeds, that the area was "bitter, envious, aggressive, impoverished, the kind of place where if you take a four quid taxi ride, you're a pampered aristocrat." That was in the '00s and perhaps it's changed a bit since he was there 'cos I wouldn't go that far. Unpretentious? Sure. Aggressive? Nah. That said, when I moved back in 2022 a number of friends did tell me they found Leeds scary and/or aggressive so maybe I just have my rose-tinted specs on when it comes to the city I love.

Across the other side of the Pennines where my mum's side of the family live is another fairly segregated area around Blackburn. I remember my grandma dropping me off at the train station after I'd been visiting, and we waited in her car as it was bitterly cold outside. Also waiting for the train were a family of headscarf-clad women, including an elderly woman, waiting for the train. A young lad in trackies came sauntering along smoking his cigarette and my grandma asked me if we should invite him to stay warm in the car with us. I replied: "Really, Grandma? What about that old lady?!" After some initial trepidation, she agreed to invite the family in, who proceeded to huddle in the back as we all giggled nervously at our newfound companionship.

But not all interactions end so well. A *Panorama* programme about Blackburn named 'White Fright' was made first in 2007, then returned a decade later. In 2017 there were 100,000 white Brits and 40,000 Asian Brits, many of whom are Muslim, with the number of white people ever decreasing as they left and Asian families replaced them: a phenomenon known as 'white flight'. Residents from both sides of the divide were interviewed with some simply stating that "they live in their areas, we live in our areas," while others felt threatened: "They'll take over eventually... they'll take our culture." I'm not sure where they'd be taking it, but it seems to be a common concern. That said, Blackburn comedian Tez Ilyas joked that if British culture involves "going to another country, not speaking the language, sticking to your own religion, forcing your customs on others and making no effort to integrate... according to the bigots, Muslims are the main people upholding it."

Integration in Blackburn is complicated, with some for it, and others actively discouraging their children from mixing with people from the other community. The push factor for some white folks came when the local pubs started to close down as many Muslims don't drink, leading business to ebb away like a hole in a beer barrel. In 1937, Orwell wrote of the slum clearances taking housing further from pubs: "for a working-class population, which uses the pub as a kind of club, it is a serious blow at communal life." When my parents were moving from my childhood home, my dad would often reject houses on the premise that "it's lovely but not exactly walking distance from t' pub." My sister's love for the pub was at one point so great that she moved in above one with the manager. So, Orwell's observation still holds truth today.

I've heard grievance at pubs being lost as a result of Asian neighbours myself. On a 2024 flight to Spain, I sat next to a man from Stalybridge, who was on a lads' trip to Benidorm. He told me there used to be about twenty pubs on a two-mile road in his town, complaining half were now "Asian shops". I got the feeling he assumed I would commiserate, but I replied that he could now get curry as well as a pint, so had the best of both worlds. He didn't seem convinced and I didn't have the energy to point out how Benidorm is basically a British enclave, just thought it passive aggressively, like a good Brit.

Attempts to integrate children educated in separate Blackburn schools have included school trips to meet one another and participate in sports days, as well as more English language learning opportunities for children and families. That said, Professor Ted Candle commented that Nadiya Hussain winning the *Great British Bake Off* did more for British Muslims than ten years of government policies, which is telling. That was 2015 and she now hosts a cooking show and was invited to make the Queen's ninetieth birthday cake. She has also been open about suffering with anxiety since she was a child, writing a children's book addressing the issue, as well as discussing the struggles and successes of her arranged marriage, and how her decision to wear a headscarf was simply to "cover up her bad hair". That said, Nikesh Shukla argues in a collection of essays called *The Good Immigrant* that people of colour are often seen as "job stealers, benefit-scroungers, girlfriend-thieves" until popular culture allows them to become "good immigrants" through "winning races, baking good cakes, being conscientious doctors" (or, I'd add, being humorous commentators of pop culture like the hilarious Siddiqui family on *Gogglebox*). As much as I agree that running fast and baking well deserve celebrating, if white Brits get to simply exist in mediocrity without being the best at anything, we should defend the rights of others to be held to the same standards.

Nadiya's *Bake Off* win coincided with the murmurings of Brexit, which came along to stir the pot after some people were not happy that, between 2006 and 2014, European immigration soared. The highest number of people came from Romania and Bulgaria, followed by Western Europe then Central and Eastern Europe in general. Opposition (and certain tabloid newspapers) took the opportunity to scapegoat immigrants for the financial crisis being felt in the UK, and both European immigrants as well as people born here but who happened not to be white got yelled at to "go home" leading up to and after the referendum in 2016. In Lancashire, hate crimes against people of colour and/or anyone with an accent went up by a third – and these are only the ones that were reported and documented.

Commenting on the UK's anti-immigrant stance, comedian Kae Kurd, whose parents came to the UK as Iraqi refugees in the 1990s, made the fair point that "we call ourselves Great Britain then get surprised when people turn up to see how great it is." That said, in the collection *Displaced: Refugee Writers on Refugee Lives*, writer Marina Lewycka, who came to the UK from the former Soviet Union, adds: "My parents had sought refuge in one country – the tolerant and generous Britain of the NHS, the BBC, Oxfam, free cod-liver oil and orange juice for the young, free milk and meals in school, good wages ensured by strong trade unions, and Yorkshire neighbourliness... It feels now as though I am destined to live out my days in a very different country – a Britain of austerity, private provision, short term contracts and the minimum wage, a crude and violent language in the popular press..." There appears to be something of a cause and effect – and one of the reasons the Leave campaign left a bitter taste in many a mouth – as discussions of EU inefficiency seemed to me overshadowed by a UK "pride" that seemed to veil undercurrents of racism and a mindset of British exceptionalism which hinted at a colonial hangover.

Now, before anyone who voted to leave gets defensive, I'm not saying if you voted this way you're racist or secretly wish we could start a new colonial rampage. Arguments about far off bureaucracy were not unreasonable and it makes sense for people to want to govern themselves as locally as possible – particularly those for which politics as usual has not been working. I just don't trust the masterminds behind the idea as far as I could throw them (which is not very far as I have a dodgy elbow). I also believe that Brexit emboldened the minority in this country who are racist in the sense of wishing this country was as white as the clouds that cover our sun-deprived isles. As well as the rise in hate crimes, the situation took another violent turn in 2016 when Yorkshirewoman Jo Cox, Oxfam-worker-turned-MP, was shot and stabbed multiple times on her way to meet constituents in Batley. The attacker was a neo-Nazi with links to the National Front and the EDL who resented her support for the EU and called her a "traitor" to white people due to her pro-immigration stance. Narratives can have dire consequences, veiled or not.

One year on, the state of affairs was not improved by the emerging Windrush Scandal. The Windrush generation, so-called after the ship *MV Empire Windrush* brought workers to the UK from the Caribbean in 1948, were a group of immigrants who arrived up until the early '70s. Nearly half a million people ended up on our windy shores to be labourers, bus conductors, and hospital orderlies. The scandal was a culmination of the Tory government's 'hostile environment' policy for immigrants of 2012 which meant that landlords, workers in the NHS and banks, as well as other service providers were tasked with helping to enforce immigration controls. In other words, asked to be Big Brother for the powers that be. By 2018, many people from the Windrush generation who'd come over on their parents' passports were suddenly being declared 'illegal' if they didn't have papers, being denied access to housing and healthcare, and were arrested and faced deportation despite having spent their lives here working and paying taxes.

Word got out, and people both in the UK and the Caribbean rallied their support. At the end of 2019, a project was set up in Moss Side, Manchester, called the 'Windrush Wonders Oral History Project', to document this generation's stories to ensure people felt heard and their experiences were not forgotten. The project leaders reported that, despite PM Theresa May's eventual apology for her government's unfair treatment, many people were scared to talk in case the Home Office got wind and came to take them away. There was also an online community, 'We Are Moss Side', that was created as an "expression of solidarity" after discussions at Manchester's Windrush Centre, aimed at communicating what is "ordinary and great" about the neighbourhood, countering the idea of Moss Side as "just a story you read years ago"; a story that has, at times, been less than flattering thanks to what they call "lazy journalism".

Literature, libraries and museums are playing their part to retell modern stories of a multicultural North. On a recent trip along the western part of Hadrian's Wall, we came across another initiative aimed at inclusivity in Carlisle's Tullie Museum. As well as a 'Black Memories Matter' project documenting black history in the area, there was a 'Living Frontiers' exhibition on border walls around the world, a nod to the nearby wall and the city's long history as a border town. Visitors could leave tags with a message on a piece of wire fence and, amongst kind words written by children, there were a couple of "Save Ukraine" tags and a "Free Palestine". Despite one museum reviewer arguing that the steep entrance fee prevented working-class folks from accessing the info middle-class folk already know, I thought it was a testament to one Northern city's attempt to educate and inspire thought through local history on a topic so often fraught with tension and assumptions on both sides. Especially timely as all we've heard in the news in 2023 is the then government banging on about "stopping the boats" to prevent people reaching British shores to seek safety. (They did actually float the idea – if you'll pardon the pun – of building a wall out in the Channel in 2020, though it never materialised).

If we were inclined to be the kind of people that look for

a silver lining to every cloud, we could say the pandemic high-lighted how, instead of being benefit-scroungers, immigrants are in fact a vital part of society. Many refugees volunteered for the NHS as cleaners and, as well as the Captain Tom Moore who walked around his garden a hundred times to raise money for the health service, centenarian Daburil Choudhury (who came from Bangladesh to study English Literature in the '50s) walked too, despite fasting during Ramadan. The pandemic also highlighted the importance of immigrants to our NHS as 20 per cent of care workers (triple that for London) and a quarter of all hospital staff are immigrants, including many doctors and nurses, speaking two hundred languages between them. According to *The Guardian*, five thousand nurses went back to other EU countries as a result of the Brexit vote, leaving student nurses to plug the gaps when the pandemic blew into town.

As well as depending on immigrants for our health service, a fifth of agricultural workers are immigrants and half of food production workers. When the pandemic hit, British farmers were left imploring Brits to pick fruit for them as they had lost the usual Eastern European workers they relied on. So, there are many arguments as to why immigration is not only not a bad thing, but why it is actively a positive thing (and I don't just mean for their labour). Evidence has shown that immigration actually boosts productivity and innovation and can promote regeneration, particularly in areas with ageing populations and economic deprivation as immigrants can stimulate supply and demand for services and are usually of working age. There were almost 20,000 international students enrolled in Northeastern universities in the academic year of 2014-2015, contributing £244 million to these institutions, alongside another £213 million spent off-campus. But aside from appealing to capitalist sentiments by pointing out that immigrants contribute monetarily, social justice would argue that we kind of have an overdue IOU to a large proportion of the world due to a colonial past in which the giving and taking ratio did not quite balance out.

There's also the simple but important argument that there is beauty and strength in diversity. You may be wondering why I, a white woman who's told you all her family are from the North, decided to write a chapter on immigration. Aside from the fact that anyone can – and, hopefully, should? – care about the stories of people who might not share an ethnic identity (but will share other identities), I've been a migrant a number of times over outside the UK, and I often work with migrants in the North as an educator. On one unusually sunny day in 2023 I took my class on a walk to map the local Leeds neighbourhood. When we got to the first shop, a Muslim Algerian women explained what halal meant to the Christian Ukrainians and translated the Arabic for us. When we reached another shop with an alphabet we didn't recognise, an Eritrean guy informed us it was his native language, Tigrinya, and explained the cultural artefacts in the shop window. Along the way, they asked me about the meaning behind some graffiti on the walls or questions about other areas of the city. At the beginning of the course with these students I asked them what they wanted to learn, and they all said 'British culture', as they believed it was important for them to know in order to integrate into their new home. But integration is a two-way process and in a superdiverse city like Leeds, urban 'Britishness' is multicultural, so we can learn from one another.

It could be argued that the globalisation of people and products has done its share of damage as well as good, but I still dislike current narratives pitting of one group of working people against another by spreading fear, as well as the incorrect assumption that anyone north of the Watford Gap "likes an ale and hates immigrants."[19]

Whilst the idea of 'Northerners' used to conjure images of white men in flat caps and women in pinnies, it now includes brown women in headscarves and black girls with braids. I'm proud that people from all over have been able to make the North their home, against the often-stacked odds. And, as much as I love pasties and Bond movies, I'm glad I can also appreciate pizza and curry; Persian rugs and Mexican murals; the movie *Amélie* and the writing of Eduardo Galeano; idioms in different languages and music from around the world. Immigration expands the limits of our world without us having to go anywhere (as well as precisely because we did, historically, go almost everywhere) showing us "potentially infinite ways of living at home abroad or abroad at home that have developed as a result of human migrations."[20] At the risk of sounding trite, the fact that our planet is so varied is what makes it so interesting, if we can respect instead of fear our differences – while understanding that we still have much in common. What's more, understanding our colonial ties reminds us why the North has become home to so many people from around the world. And at the risk of sounding idealistic, since the adage says we fear that which we don't understand, to move beyond this we could draw on Northern neighbourliness and working-class solidarity to learn from, and support, one another. While politician Margaret Thatcher argued there existed only individuals and families, working-class Cockney director Joan 'The Mother of Modern Theatre' Littlewood believed in community, insisting this wasn't romanticism (and we could probably do to listen to more artists than politicians).

As integration in communities means adaptation from both newcomers and those already here, if we value diversity as we profess to as a nation, we would do well to remember this as we continue our never-ending task of making and re-making the region we know and love.

VIII. Good Morning, Mr Magpie

I didn't know why I had always been superstitious until I read a book called *It's an Old Lancashire Custom,* which stated that Lancashire folk "feel bewildered when we meet people with no supernatural traditions". Aha! I thought. It was in my blood to believe in spirits and sprites, ghouls and goblins, witches and wizards.

Despite being a person who values science and logic, I have always been drawn to the supernatural. I wouldn't say I was superstitious, but certainly a bit 'stitious'. Growing up, my mum always had a plant in the house called 'honesty' which, not surprisingly, is said to bring honesty, truth and wealth to your home. When my sister moved into her first family house, honesty was gifted to her. It's called a 'silver dollar plant' in the USA. As a child, if I spilled salt, I always threw some over my shoulder (right over left), made sure my umbrella was down before stepping inside a house, didn't walk under ladders, and still 'touch wood' to ward away any misfortune that might be lurking, lest optimism gets the better of me. Some stranger superstitions in Northern history include not singing before breakfast if you didn't want to cry before bed; not setting your cups facing one another in case they gossiped about the family; and, according to Yorkshire housewives of old, believing that bread would not rise if there was a corpse nearby. Let's hope there's not many restaurants near graveyards or those Yorkshire puds will be disappointing.

The aforementioned book by Corbridge talks of the many spirits – or 'boggarts' as they were called across Lancashire and Yorkshire, named after the bogs of the peatlands from which they emerged – that would terrorise unsuspecting locals. "If you were very unlucky, you might even meet Trash or Skriker on your way home" the "king of shaggy dogs, a huge beast whose red eyes often glared through the night in the Burnley district."[21]

Trash featured in Charlotte Brontë's *Jane Eyre* when Jane mistook Mr Rochester's dog and then horse for the beast that haunts lonely travellers. Rochester also asks Jane if she bewitched his horse to fall with help from "the men in green". Other ghouls terrorising local inhabitants included Peg Powler, a green-haired water hag who lived in the River Tees and snatches away children who come too close to the water in County Durham. And in 1890, it was reported that a Manchester woman confused a yellow boggart with an escaped zoo lion. Other boggarts, however, would help families out. One Blackburn farm apparently had a ghoul "who deserved union rates of pay"[22] for milking the cows and harnessing the horses and so on.

In case you encountered an angry rather than industrious sprite, folks had various ways to ward off evil. Hanging horseshoes above your front door was one such method, a tradition thought to have roots in Irish folklore as far back as 959 AD. As a kid, I scooped up a horseshoe I found on the road in the village and my mum told me that hanging them above the door was good luck, though neither of us knew its ghostly origins. I had it balanced on my bedroom door frame for years, leading my mum to joke that it would end up being bad luck for whoever's head it eventually fell on. The horseshoe now adorns my sister's back door (sensibly nailed in there), I suppose in case the spirits get wise to the front doors being protected and try to sneak in the back.

Turns out it's not only me who's hanging on to some of those old beliefs, as a 2017 poll of Northeasterners revealed 76 per cent consider themselves superstitious, with cracking a mirror being the most common fear, followed by counting magpies, and avoiding walking under ladders or opening brollies indoors. When I see a single magpie, I usually stop what I'm doing, frantically scanning the area for more black and white feathers. This happened on a walk the other day and, in my search, took my eyes off the ground and tripped over a protruding tree root. Recovering my upright posture (and remaining dignity), I couldn't decide if this was proof of the magpie's power, or evidence that superstition can make you fall flat on your face. My friend's Lancastrian dad greets single magpies with "Good morning, Mr Magpie. How's your wife and father?", which apparently sidesteps the sorrow the lone avians bring, so I might try that next time instead.

My belief in the supernatural might have something to do with the fact that my hometown, Chester, has as one of its claims to fame being the most haunted city in England. Just as you can take a Roman tour around the city, you can also take a ghost tour which will tell you about the various souls that remain trapped within the ancient city walls.

Take, for example, Thornton's chocolate shop which has a ghost who, to this day will rearrange the shelves in the night, much to the shop workers' frustration. Legend has it that the ghost is that of a young eighteenth century woman who, jilted on her wedding day, hung herself and has been waiting for her groom ever since. The George and Dragon Pub allegedly has a murdered monk in the cellar and an armoured Roman soldier that guests can hear clanging about in the dead of night; and the 'Old Crypt' at Watergates Bar is haunted by murdered priests and a young girl who died during the Great Plague of 1665 when the place was used as a temporary hospital and morgue.

The most haunted building in the city is thought to be Stanley Palace, a looming black and white structure. My mum took me to do a piano exam there as a child and the cold emptiness of the space gave me the creeps and I promptly gave up lessons. I only later found out the place has the highest numbers of spirits in the city, thus encouraging my belief in a sixth sense. My mum had a different approach, saying that when she did her music exams there as an adult, she would imagine playing to the ghosts to calm her nerves. Spurred on by the numerous ghost stories of my city, and the tale of a drowning in the village pond which used to be where my childhood house stood, my friend and I were convinced one day that we had found the gravestone at the bottom of my garden, my sister also swears she and her friends saw it too. Endless sleepovers were spent scaring the crap out of ourselves with ghost stories in a house that punctuated such tales with well-timed creaking intervals.

But it's not only Chester that has its fair share of ghosts since York competes for the title of most haunted. With over five hundred recorded sightings, it has a renowned ghost in the shape of George Villiers (of Georgie Porgie nursery rhyme fame) troubling the Cock and Buttle pub, as well as Clifford's Tower which is said to turn red every year with the blood of the Jews who died there after an anti-Semitic mob attack in the twelfth century.

Other ghostly stories include a street in a Southport village called 'Ralph's Wife's Lane', named after a fisherman failed to return home one evening, his small boat wrecked at sea. His wife went looking for him, calling his name, but to no avail. Local legend has it that she can still be seen on wild and windy nights, searching for her beloved.

The supernatural can also be found in local literature such as Rochdale poet Edwin Waugh's nineteenth century poem, 'What Ails Thee, My Son Robin?'

Thi fuustep's sadly awter't, –
Aw used to know it weel, –
Neaw, arto fairy-stricken, lad;
Or, arto gradely ill?
Or, hasto bin wi' th' witches
I'th cloof, at deep o'th neet?
Come, tell mo, Robin, tell mo, –
For summat is not reet!

The verse also mentions witches and fairies which have a long history in British folklore. In Scotland, they could be spoken of as royalty, and in County Durham, fear of fairy-led child abduction was present after legend told of a girl who followed the sound of music into a fairy cave in Weardale.

When I was a child, the invoked tooth fairy would leave tiny messages on coloured heart-shaped paper in envelopes the size of a thumbnail in exchange for whatever gnasher had recently fallen out. Receiving them was magic and I kept them for years. My mum still refuses to admit it was her so, either way, I'm grateful for the charm and love held in those paper hearts. I spent countless hours checking mushrooms that sprang up under the willow tree in our garden, hoping to meet my miniature mate, though I had no such luck. (Fairy existence can be employed passive aggressively, such as when you know someone had something of yours recently and it is missing, yet they deny all knowledge of its whereabouts: "It must've been taken by t' bloody fairy then".)

Fairies popped up during the pandemic when a sprinkling of mystery emerged after intricate fairy doors appeared in the hollows of trees on various Cheshire woodland walks in what I assume was an attempt to cheer up anxious walkers. An opportunity to imagine other worlds within the woods instead of the dystopian one we were dealing with in the outside world.

Poems have also been written documenting otherworldly happenings such as eery bells rang by unseen hands:

Oft on Pendle's side one hears,
A passing sound of distant bells,
No legend old nor human wit
Can tell us whence the music swells.
'Tis thought that they, by Assheton brought
From Whalley's convent towers,
Still call at times the drowsy monks
To prayers at midnight hours.

As well as its ghostly musicians, Pendle is famous for other supernatural beings: witches. The Pendle Witch Trials (England's Salem) took place in Lancashire in 1612, sentencing twelve women to death for killing ten people with witchcraft, after the fire of suspicion was stoked by King James' *Daemonologie* book, published in 1599.

One somewhat flawed test for witchcraft was to drown a woman – if they lived, they were a witch, if they died, they were not. Over to the east, Newcastle had their own witch trials on Town Moor in 1650, with a finger pricking test. If they bled, they were innocent; if they didn't, they were a witch. But at twenty shillings a witch, I'm sure the witch-pricker didn't press very hard or used a blunt pin to keep himself in a cushty job. Thirteen women were hanged as the public looked on and cheered.

I struggle to find the words to capture the spirit of the Pendle, so instead share a description by Sylvia Corbridge that captures the hill's magic: "Pendle Hill, rising 1,500 feet out of some of the loveliest border country in the North of England, has a dramatic quality out of all proportion to its size. To walk on its slopes on a windy day, striding over knee-high grass tufts, setting your face against a breeze in which the curlews cry, is to step out of this world into a land bounded by the greyness of a twisting stone wall and the white bank of a cloud." It really does have an atmosphere you don't expect, and I'm saying that after going with expectations. It sneaks up on you with its other-worldly presence after walking up through a village which looks like any other (aside from all the witch paraphernalia). The hill also inspired a folk song called 'Old Pendle' which describes the beauty of the area, dedicating a verse to the witches:

When witches fly on a cold winter's night
We won't tell a soul and we'll bolt the door tight.
We'll sit around the fire and we'll keep ourselves warm
Until once again we can walk on your arms.

Pendle Hill is my relations' stomping ground and family legend claims that one of the accused witches, whose maiden name was Whittaker (a family surname of ours) is a distant relative. To cement my belief in our spellbinding lineage, one of the young witches shares my given name, and a 1951 book titled *Mist Over Pendle* had as its protagonist a girl named Marjorie Whittaker, which also happens to be my maternal grandmother's name. On hearing this as a child, I became convinced of my witchy blood, thus solidifying my interest in all things supernatural. I burned an abundance of candles and incense, much to my firefighter father's horror. "Give over, will ya? What will the lads say if a fireman's house burns down?!" I soon gave up my magical aspirations, however, after a love spell I did successfully landed me my first boyfriend. We had our first kiss aged eleven in a field and the sloppy encounter horrified me so much I went home and prayed to whatever deities were out there that I wouldn't have to kiss him again. The next week he wasn't in school as he'd had an accident and knocked some teeth out. I was relieved but figured I'd best give the magic malarkey a rest before anyone else got hurt.

During the first Covid lockdown, while people were working in pyjamas, baking bread, and promising themselves they'd get fit, I was foraging around and experimenting with making dandelion honey, nettle soup, and elderflower cordial (which I can highly recommend in a gin and tonic). When presenting my family with my creations, my dad would grumble: "I'm sure you're a witch. It's in t' blood", shaking his head at my mother as if she were to blame. The elder tree has long been held sacred, protected by the Elder Woman who lived in its trunk. As a result, many country folk would not cut or burn the tree for fear of upsetting her and, planted outside your home, it is said to protect from evil spirits (just don't fall asleep under one on a Midsummer's eve, as the fairies might carry you away).

As much as I'd like to think I inherited powers from a witchy ancestor, did the Pendle women simply know the secrets of the forest? Were they midwives or healers? Herbalists who offered natural remedies for common ailments (remedies included plants that induced abortions, seen as the devil's work in religious communities)? Whatever they were, I call on that Pendle Forest magic when conventional strength falls short.

It was also on Pendle Hill that a man named Fox received a vision from God and so began the Quaker religion in 1652, leading some to question whether the hill is a source of mystical energy. Fox enlisted fellow Lancastrian, Margaret Fell, to help spread the ideas across the North, often from the comfort of her home, Swarthmoor Hall. She was later imprisoned for this, where she wrote *Women's Speaking Justified*, a scripture-based argument for women's religious leadership which became a major text of its kind that century.

Other stretches of land in the North with similar

allegations include Cross Fell, the highest mountain in the North Pennines, which used to be called Fiend's Fell as it was reported to house evil spirits. So scared were the Cumbrians that an exorcism was carried out during the Middle Ages, which moved the malevolent souls only five miles down the road to what is the current Fiend's Fell, where the locals were apparently not bothered enough about their new residents to do anything about them. Apparently, mystical land does not like to be moved, either. A former housemate of mine was from Carlisle and told me that Cumbria continues to be plagued by misfortune ever since the Cursing Stone – a slab of earth with a sixteenth century curse engraved in it – was brought to one of Carlisle's museums in 2001. Since then, livestock have been wiped out by foot-and-mouth, a flood devastated the area, factories closed, and Carlisle United dropped a league. Genuine discussions have arisen over whether to revere the thing or smash it to pieces.

In North Yorkshire, alongside the River Nidd, is Old Mother Shipton's cave and petrifying well. The Old Mother became known as Knaresborough's Prophetess, predicting the fates of various rulers of her time with predictions such as: "The White King dead, the Wolf shall then/ With blood usurp the Lion's den". She also foresaw events such as the Great Fire of London in 1666. Thankfully though, she wasn't always correct as she declared that "the world to an end shall come in eighteen hundred and eighty-one."

(I searched "what happened in 1881?", just in case, and it turns out that a bomb exploded at a military barracks in Salford killing a young boy, a blizzard passed over the South, and the First Boer War raged, then ended, in South Africa.)

Raised in the cave by her fifteen-year-old mother who refused to name the father, both mother and daughter were shunned from the village. Due to her daughter's ugly looks Mother Shipton preferred to stay in the cave, studying the forest and making potions from its plants. The well near her cave has attracted visitors since 1630 due to its petrifying properties, turning objects placed there into stone within months. Today, it is rather macabrely adorned with children's teddy bears.

Science or magic? Does it matter? As Jeannette Winterson dryly pointed out, calling upon magic in dark times by sitting in a chalk circle is surely better than sitting in a gas oven. So if people want to throw a coin into a well and make a wish, maybe we should let 'em.

As well as witches, the North also has had its share of wizards knocking about.

I previously mentioned the Alderley Edge 'wizard walk' I embarked upon, emerging from the legend of King Arthur which reputes that Merlin was an unpredictable sixth century sorcerer (reportedly the product of an incubus and a Welsh nun), who guided the King throughout his reign. Many areas of the UK have their own Merlin legend, and our Cheshire tale goes something like this: Deep inside a cave in Alderley Edge lay a sleeping army of King Arthur's knights, guarded by the wizard and only to be awakened in times of great peril. All but one knight had a white mare to ride off on to confront such battles. One day a farmer was approached by an old man on his way to market with a white mare who offered to buy the horse when he prophesised that the horse would not sell in Macclesfield. The army was then complete and ready to save Cheshire as quick as they could roll out of their rocky beds. The alder tree after which the area is named has long been considered sacred in the North and witches' covens from nearby would go to the Edge to worship. At Stormy Point you can also find a gash in the rock named Devil's Grave, a shallow mine that probably yielded copper, were you brave enough to enter.

They say the devil makes work for idle hands, and the

devil himself was surely not idle as he seems to have got around quite a bit, making appearances across the North in places such as the Devil's Bridge in Kirkby Lonsdale. The bridge was built in the twelfth century, allegedly after a woman accepted the devil's help to build it so she could get across the fast-flowing river to retrieve her cow. The devil agreed but on the condition that he would receive the soul of the first being to cross the bridge but, instead of crossing herself, she threw a bun on the bridge so her dog ran after it. The devil, offered a canine, slunk away defeated.

Of course, the devil didn't limit his visitations to the North: the South has the Devil's Dyke in Sussex, Devil's Point in Plymouth, and the curiously named Devil's Punch Bowl in Surrey. Wales has its own Devil's Bridge, Scotland a rock formation named the Devil's Pulpit, and Northern Ireland has a seaside cave called the Devil's Churn. Nor did Beelzebub show British favouritism as Argentina has the Devil's Throat at the Iguazu Falls; South Africa has the Devil's Peak; and the US seems as worried as us Brits about Satan with the Devil's Corkscrew in the Grand Canyon; their own Devil's Bridge in Arizona, another Devil's Punchbowl in Oregon, a Devil's Kettle waterfall in Minnesota, and Devil's Lake in Wisconsin. I visited the latter in 2019 and learned that the original name of the lake was 'Spirit Lake'. So what happened? The lake was formerly named by the indigenous people of the area who regarded the water as sacred but, after settlers arrived to claim the land, they got scared of the noises heard echoing from the surrounding rock and decided the place was haunted.

Back in the North of England, the land has been plagued by another kind of demon hybrid, the vampire. Whitby Abbey appears in Bram Stoker's fabled gothic novel *Dracula* ('dracula' meaning 'devil' in the Wallachian language, with inspiration drawn from the Romanian Prince, Vlad the Impaler). In it, a character records in her diary a legend that a lady in white could be seen in one of the windows in the ruins of Whitby Abbey. In the scene that made the Abbey famous, the shape-shifting Dracula ascended the one hundred and ninety-nine steps to Whitby's St Mary's Church graveyard in the form of a black dog.

Elsewhere in Yorkshire, Wharram Percy is a mysterious village, abandoned shortly after 1500. According to a 2017 study by Historic England and Southampton University, bodies were found decapitated, and the bones of the dead mutilated and burned to stop corpses rising from their graves, spreading disease, or assaulting the living. Researchers believe that the restless corpses were thought to be a result of lingering malevolent forces in those who'd committed evil deeds when alive, so I'm guessing the town must've had its share of sinners. Northern writer, Adam Ferrar, on the other hand argued that monsters perhaps like the area as there are numerous remote spots where you can mutilate in peace.

Superstition runs deep across the region, and it doesn't stop with fairies and ghosts, or witches and vampires. The North has other mythical monsters such as a Cumbrian legend about werewolves. Except since we haven't had any wolves knocking about since the 15th century, the legend was about weresheep. The story goes that a girl named Belle Sheephead found her pet lamb killed by a fox but, instead of crying over spilt blood, she drank it. By the time the next full moon showed its face on the Lakeland fells, she had transformed into a weresheep, stalking unfortunate people travelling over the hills. I'm assuming Sheephead was a name given to her after the fact, or else that is one heavy case of a self-fulfilling prophecy.

Cheshire author Alan Garner's family have been around Alderley Edge for three hundred years and the local legends were passed on by his blacksmith grandfather. His books – many of which are set in Cheshire – reflect such folklore.

Garner also wrote a collection of folk tales from all over the world, explaining that we humans have always tried to make sense of the natural world by turning aspects into gods or devils or spirits or animals. He argued that although we sometimes explain such forces by rules we call 'magic', he would call such magic 'the science we have not discovered yet.'" It may be true that the witches were ordinary women in the wrong place at the wrong time, that Fox received his vision from God after walking for days without food or water, that the petrifying well water has an unusually high mineral content, and that Mother Shipton died over one hundred years before her Fire of London prediction – wait long enough and your visions of a city built of timber and thatch burning to the ground might come true. But I prefer to live in a world that holds onto a little bit of mystery and magic, upholding the traditions of my ancestors.

IX. We're All Mad Here

As a child I was known for two things. One was being able to fall asleep anywhere (resting places include the backdoor step, half in, half out, as well as leaning against a post in line for a theme park ride). The other was always having my face in a book (unless I was in the car as that would've ended badly for everyone in the vehicle).

Although I devoured books at my local library from a young age, I was never given – nor did I know who to ask – any directions on what to read. For the first half of my life, I simply read whatever caught my eye (from the US's *Sweet Valley High* to Melvin Burgess's *Junk*). Heading towards adulthood, I decided I should read the 'classics', thinking that I needed to know what (I thought) everyone else knew. And by 'everyone else' I mean smart people in faraway newspapers or magazines, as no one in my life was talking about these books. I only later learned that these lists were created by and for middle-class readers, and I'd been unknowingly buying into the idea that 'knowledge' or 'culture' only existed within such pages.

Similarly recommended by the media I was consuming, I then started reading books from around the world, learning about Nigeria's history in Chimamanda Ngozi Adichie's *Purple Hibiscus* or about postcolonial Chile in Isabel Allende's *The House of the Spirits* (still a favourite). But when I wanted to learn about my own family's working-class history – the roots of where I came from – I didn't really know where to start. Of the books we'd been made to read in school, not one of the authors had been Northern. At GCSE I remember *Romeo and Juliet* (we'd all seen the Baz Luhrmann movie so anything without Leonardo DiCaprio kind of felt like a disappointment), *Lord of the Flies* (a bunch of posh boys get stranded then things get ugly), and *The Curious Incident of the Dog in the Night-Time* (neurodivergent kid investigates a canine murder and it's wonderful). Despite my love for reading, I declined to choose English Lit as an A Level as spending hours discussing what the author meant in their sentence about a moving curtain kind of sucked the joy out of books for me. Maybe it was just windy that day, Miss. Nowadays kids still get Shakespeare – we're not getting rid of him any time soon – but also Simon Armitage's poems and a choice of the plays *A Taste of Honey*, *The History Boys*, or *Blood Brothers*.

Despite being historically overlooked on this national scale, Northern literature has had a lot to offer. From unruly passion on moody wind-swept moors to everyday struggles in run-down industrial towns, it would be fair to say that such art has been influenced by the land it encompasses and the history that infuses it. Much has been written about the 'hard times' of the North, as well as a variety of literature from and about the North that doesn't centre around slag heaps and destitution. Daniel Dafoe wrote *Robinson Crusoe* during his time spent in Gateshead in 1719 and *Goldilocks and the Three Bears* was written in Keswick by poet Robert Southey who adapted a traditional tale for the (then) modern taste in 1837. Bradfordian J. B. Priestley's 1934 *English Journey* was of a similar vein (and the same publisher) to George Orwell's *Road to Wigan Pier*, which also described the state of the industrialised country as a plea for socialism – allegedly helping Labour to get elected in 1945.

Author Frances Wilson wrote in *The New Statesman* that the South was literature's finishing school, while the North undid decorum where people stopped talking 'properly' and became themselves – such as with Mary Lennox's secret garden transforming her from nasty to nice. She went on to argue that while the South was about preserving what you already had, the North was a place of "courage and transformation". There were, however, those who wanted to preserve parts of the North exactly as they already were; those who knew and loved its countryside. The most famous Northern poet of the nineteenth century had to be William Wordsworth, born and raised in the Lake District, later living in Cambridge and Paris, then choosing to return to the rural idyll of Cumbria. Wordsworth moved to Grasmere with his sister when he was twenty-nine and had many artists and poets over at Dove Cottage. He declared the area "the loveliest spot that man hath ever found." The seeds for his ubiquitous daffodil poem were planted in 1802 by his walks through the countryside with his sister and, not far off in Helvellyn, an incident inspired a somewhat less delicate poem. A young artist fell to his death on a walk with his dog in 1805 and three months later, his body was found with his terrier waiting faithfully by his side. Of the incident, Wordsworth wrote:

How long didst thou think that his
silence was slumber?
When the wind waved his garment,
how oft didst thou start?

Novelist Priestley wrote that Northerners "have to make an effort to appreciate a poet like Shelley, with his rather gassy enthusiasm and his bright Italian colouring; but we have Wordsworth in our very legs." I am unsure of what it means to have a dead poet in one's legs, but it manages to sound both spiritual and down to earth.

To the east, a family of writers by the name of Brontë moved to Haworth in 1820 and the three sisters published various novels under male pseudonyms. This necessity was because women were believed to only good for embroidering and curtseying, not for having original thoughts or opinions or imagination. Of classic English literature, one of my favourites has to be Charlotte's *Jane Eyre,* published in 1847. While Jane Austen's character one-eighties frustrated me in the ever-popular story of love amongst the landed gentry, *Pride and Prejudice*, I preferred to root for plain Jane and her complicated feelings for Mr Rochester as she struggled through life, trying to find her place. I could see myself in Jane when I first read the book as a moody teenager, as I felt at times quiet and overlooked; more so than in the pampered wealthy ladies with their dresses and delicate speech in other classic novels I'd read up to then. Years later, I scooped Charlotte's *The Professor* in a second-hand book shop after visiting Cheshire's Tatton Park estate which, although slightly tedious (the book, not the park), dramatises the writer's own adventures as a teacher overseas, which was something I could also relate to as a woman who'd moved abroad to teach.

Sister Emily Brontë knocked out her own classic about Cathy and Heathcliff's made-for-each-other madness in *Wuthering Heights* which, according to gossip, was based on some publications about Wordsworth and his sister, Dorothy, written by Mancunian Thomas de Quincey in 1837. Despite my love for the non-traditional protagonist and gothic undertones in *Jane Eyre*, I couldn't get on board with

Wuthering Heights as I struggled to find a character I could identify with – or even like – and everything felt a little too oppressive (though maybe that was the point, in which case Emily gets full marks for atmosphere on that moody moor).

Charlotte's *Jane Eyre*, Emily's *Wuthering Heights*, and Anne's *Agnes Grey* were all published in 1847, making it a pretty successful year for the sisters. We had in my childhood home a massive Brontë tome with the above two novels plus *Agnes Grey* and *Villette*, though I have yet to tackle the latter pair. When I asked my mum what *Agnes Grey* is about, she replied that she couldn't remember but that it was "miserable" and that only *Villette*, a reworking of Charlotte's earlier *Professor*, was worth reading. (Can you see where I get my literary critique skills from?) I then turned elsewhere for input on *Agnes Grey* and was told it was about a mistreated governess working for the landed gentry so added it to my 'to read' list, but I'll have to get back to you with more misery analysis when I get around to reading it myself.

The surrounding gloom of the moors of the Brontë residence of course seeped into the sister's morose regional stories, and it was suggested that their servants' superstitions and folk tales were also an influence for the appearance of ghostly figures. As well as the surrounding people and environment, their tragic childhoods similarly contributed to the gothic "misery" in their writing as their mother died when they were young, perhaps due to complications after the birth of the girls' youngest sister, Anne; followed by their two older sisters, Maria and Elizabeth, who died from tuberculosis after contracting it at school; their father was something of a recluse for whom the sisters had to look after in adulthood due to sickness; and their poet brother Branwell struggled with substance abuse from which he ultimately died too. Then, like a stack of unfortunate dominoes, Emily caught a cold at Branwell's funeral which led to her demise (though a housemaid declared that she'd died of a broken heart after her brother's passing). Emily's death in turn caused suffering to Anne, who sickened and died shortly after of consumption. Charlotte was the last to go in 1855 with her unborn child, less than a month before her thirty-ninth birthday, possibly due to morning sickness-related dehydration. That said, it has been alleged that the sisters spent their lives drinking water contaminated by runoff from the nearby graveyard. If that isn't a suitably gothic ending, I don't know what is. The Brontë parsonage house in Haworth can now be visited as a museum, run by the Brontë Society, one of the world's oldest literary societies founded in 1893 and a literary mecca for visitors from around the world. Just don't drink the tap water (I joke).

The first biography about Charlotte Brontë was written by Elizabeth Gaskell, a writer born in London but sent to live with her deceased mother's family in Cheshire. Although she originally wrote short stories under a male pseudonym of Cotton Mather Mills (an appropriate alias), Gaskell settled in Manchester with her husband, writing *North and South* in 1854 under her married name, loosely based on her own experience as a Southerner moving to 'Milton' (mill town... get it?) The story, sometimes called a "condition of England" novel, depicts the mill owners battling workers' strikes (as well as a Mr Darcy-esque love story where a guy who at first seems like a bit of a twat turns out to be all noble in the end). The book was made into a 2004 BBC series with an evocative opening credit of the mills, white with snow-like cotton floating through the air; the same 'snow' that wrecked many a working child's lungs. That same year, Hampshire-born prolific writer Charles Dickens published *Hard Times*, his only novel not to have scenes set in London. The book (and various screen adaptations) is set in Coketown, which some argue is Manchester, others Preston. The novel followed the idea that 'you reap what you sow', satirising industrialisation and the social ills that accompany it. Moving from isolation on the moors to life in the cities, grim industrial novels such as these gave the rest of the country an insight into (and critique of) industrialisation in the North and the effects on the people working inside its factories.

From the harsh realities of country and city life to a playful fantasy in an entirely fabricated realm, in 1865 Lewis Carroll wrote one of my favourite childhood tales, *Alice's Adventures in Wonderland*. There is much wisdom to be found amidst the absurd and, when Alice plunged down a hole in her garden after chasing a waistcoat-clad rabbit, she asked the Cheshire Cat for directions: "Would you tell me, please, which way I ought to go from here?" He replied, sensibly: "That depends a good deal on where you want to get to". The grinning feline later cheerfully informed Alice "we're all mad here" as she navigated a plethora of weird and wonderful characters in a topsy-turvy world. My friend, who studied English Lit at uni, told me that, though the book falls under the "literary nonsense" genre, she insists it should instead be catalogued under "drug-fuelled". But no matter how the characters came about, they remain in our national psyche today in the form of film remakes, paraphernalia, and Wonderland-themed cafes.

In honour of Carroll's riddlesome moggy, there's a pub in my hometown and a Cheshire-brewed blonde ale named after him. A childhood souvenir of mine is a worn-out leather bookmark from a book shop commemorating a visit to Daresbury, in the Borough of Halton, Carroll's birthplace. Carroll called the village "the happy spot where I was born" and it is certainly a pretty place with woodland canal walks (as well as some nice little Range Rovers and convertibles knocking about). Despite this claim to fame, the Carroll family moved to North Yorkshire when Lewis was eleven after his Anglican father was given a rectory in Croft-on-Tees. It is apparently in the garden here, under a now gnarled acacia tree, that Oxford-educated Carroll put his characters on paper. In addition to a Disney animation made in the '50s, Tim Burton resurrected the tale in 2010 with Johnny Depp as the Mad Hatter and Helen Bonham-Carter as the Queen of Hearts. I wish I could say I loved it but I'm happy to stick to the book or the cartoon: if it in't broke, don't fix it.

Another writer of timeless anthropomorphic children's stories, Beatrix Potter, was an only child who spent most of her time playing with animals. Despite growing up in London, both of her parents were from around Manchester and she often holidayed in the Lake District, eventually moving there where she married aged forty-seven after having written numerous books, twenty-three of which her well-known children's books. Potter wrote and illustrated the much-loved 1901 *The Tale of Peter Rabbit* with his friends such as Mrs Tiggy-Winkle and Jemima Puddle-Duck; all while writing illustrated papers on botany (that had to be introduced by men as women could not attend academic meetings) and being a prize-winning breeder of the local Herdwick sheep. Beatrix's childhood home was destroyed in the Blitz, but her seventeenth century Hill Top farmhouse can be visited as a museum after she apparently left instructions on how it was to be organised as a "time capsule of her life". Generations of kids have grown up with these characters and, if the National Trust is to be believed, one of her books is sold every fifteen seconds, over a century after their first publication.

The twentieth century also brought with it *The Railway Children*, a 1906 novel which was adapted into a classic British film in 1970. The movie was shot in Keighley and was a staple in my household growing up. The story revolves around three children from London who are forced to hide away in a house called Three Chimneys up in deepest, darkest Yorkshire (where no one will ever find you, the idea went). Much of their time is taken up with the nearby Oakworth Station railway and the people it brings them in contact with. I grew up on Station Lane, now an out of use train stop, but I would imagine myself in the film, about to stumble upon my next adventure with my friends as we scrambled over the gate to the tracks. I can report, however, that I never found anything more exciting than some village lads mucking about.

Shortly after followed *The Secret Garden*, a 1911 novel set in Yorkshire with a 1993 film adaptation which was another childhood favourite of mine. The film used the county's Allerton Castle for the exterior shots and Misselthwaite Manor for the interior and was based on the story of a spoiled young girl, unhappy and newly orphaned, and her discovery of a 'secret garden' that she brings back to life. What child wouldn't want a hidden corner of Yorkshire to call their own? I remember becoming obsessed with having my own secret garden but my dad wouldn't let me transform the dump at the bottom of our garden into my own private idyll. I tried to settle on making a modest rock garden by the house instead, but was banned from doing this as well. Undeterred, I snuck out in the night with a kitchen spoon which I used to dig the ground as the shed was locked and I persevered with my creation. I don't know if my dad was more livid about me digging up his garden or my mum about me using her spoon to do it (it's still in her cutlery drawer though and can be identified by the curved metal edge which looks like something has nibbled on the end. We don't throw away in our household...)

The inspiration and setting of the bonny beck were then replaced by the kitchen sink through a series of post-war novels dealing with twentieth century issues such as social mobility in *Room at the Top* in 1957, which was quickly followed by dreams of life in the big city in *Billy Liar* in 1959, then swapping the pit for the pitch in *This Sporting Life* in 1960. All were made into films, some of which became cult classics. *A Room at the Top* was made for the big screen in 1959, set in the West Riding of Yorkshire and following an ambitious man leaving a small factory town to make it big. On Northern stereotypes, author John Braine said on Radio 4 that if he hadn't written *A Room at the Top*, the film wouldn't have been made, and the myth wouldn't have solidified. "For the purpose of the film, only the harsher aspects of the northern landscape were essential; those high chimneys, those smoke-blackened stone buildings, those precipitous cobbled streets had a life of their own. The clear river effervescent with fish, the woods and pastures encircling the town and the moors and hills beyond – all this, and much more, had to be left out." *Billy Liar* was also made into a film, using Leeds and Bradford as the backdrop, beginning with the words: "Good morning, housewives!"

Which led me to question, is it a good morning for the housewives? Where are their stories? Watching Billy's interactions with his parents was like watching my teen years on repeat being told not to "answer back" or "be so cheeky" and laments of "what are we gonna do wi' you?" At first, I thought I could relate to his daydreaming, his preference for living in a fantasy world, as well as his resolve to get up earlier to start writing that novel. I quickly changed my mind as I don't identify with being a responsibility-dodging bigamist, drugging women's coffees to try to get my end away. Nor do I imagine taking people out with a machine gun when I don't get my own way. This story of frustrated class aspirations was also a glorified display of selfish masculinity as he ditched women left right and centre, as well as his poor old mum minutes after his grandma shuffled the mortal coil.

Poet Simon Armitage falls on the side that most films are secondary in nature to the books they are based on, though he offers *Kes* as an exception to this rule. Ken Loach's film is based on Barry Hines' 1968 *A Kestrel for a Knave* written a year earlier, set in a Yorkshire mining town, filmed in and around Hoyland, Hines's hometown. The story tells of a boy, another Billy, who finds a kestrel in a farm nest, the relationship that develops between them, and the freedom that bird represents for the boy. Armitage argues that the story creates a world somewhere between heaven and hell, with hell to be found in the coal pits and heaven a bird in flight. I haven't read the book but found the film depressing as anything. Watching the school scenes as a teacher was painful, as pedagogy back then seemed to consist of yelling and denigrating, prompting Billy to state matter-of-factly: "They're not bothered about us and we're not bothered about them." My parents confirmed this was pretty much the educational approach in their schools too, which might explain a lot about a generation of angry Boomers.

All these stories tell the tale of dissatisfied males, yearning for more in life. I was left wanting to know if their girlfriends or sisters or mothers felt the same. Was the country not ready for an angsty female protagonist? A story about Billy Liar's lover, Liz, the globetrotting, sexually liberated chain-smoker who did hop the train to London on a whim when Billy chickened out? I went digging about and stumbled across a feminist socialist author called Winifred Holtby, who Virginia Woolf described as a "Yorkshire farmer's daughter who learned to read while feeding the pigs." Holtby was credited with addressing issues such as birth control at a time where it wasn't openly discussed, writing *South Riding*, which was sadly not published until sixth months after her death in 1936. I heard *South Riding* described as what might have happened had Jane Eyre got involved in local politics, so I promptly ordered the book for it to get buried under my ever-growing 'to read' pile. I did have a peek at the BBC miniseries though, with the title character played by Yorkshire's Anna Maxwell Martin, whose face you can see in numerous Northern credits.

Then, joining the kitchen sink dramas, I found *A Taste of Honey*, originally a play by Shelagh Delaney in 1959, then made into a film in 1961. Set in Delaney's native Salford, the story touches on issues of class, race, gender, and sexual orientation as our schoolgirl protagonist, Jo, gets ditched by her mother for her latest lover, falls in love with a black sailor, finds out she's pregnant after he has already sailed away, and shacks up with a gay lad who was chucked out of his place for bringing a fella back.

(Fun fact: The Smiths have borrowed various lines as lyrics in their songs, but I can't tell you what they are because quoting song lyrics is expensive).

Twenty years later, a 1980 play written by Lancashire's Willy Russell, *Educating Rita*, also centred a woman and her dreams of upward mobility, as well as her husband's attempt to thwart them. The story follows a working-class hairdresser from Liverpool whose aspirations lead her to study an Open University course under the tutelage of a jaded, and kind of alcoholic, professor. Russell himself was a hairdresser who quit to go back to school, though he says he never had that "chip-on-the-shoulder, knee-jerk, damn the middle-classes reaction." The play was made into a successful 1983 film starring Michael Caine and Julie Walters. Russell also wrote the musical *Blood Brothers*, a story set in '60s Liverpool about twins separated at birth, one boy growing up poor and the other given to a rich family as the working-class mum couldn't afford to look after them both. What followed was the unfolding of the nature-nurture debate as one man becomes a councillor and the other ends up in prison.

Northern writers talking about the North can sometimes be written off as provincial talents but, as Melvyn Bragg says,

"I've always liked viewing the world through a grain of sand, it's sometimes the sharpest way to see it."

One such Northern writer is Leeds' Alan Bennett. Bennett wrote a series of monologues called *Talking Heads* which *The Guardian* described as a masterclass in storytelling. First broadcast in 1988, they were resurrected for the BBC in 2020 with soliloquies by numerous great British talents including the queen of Northern actresses, Sarah Lancaster (who is indeed from Lancashire), and Jodie Comer, the Scouser known for her impressive range of accents of *Killing Eve* fame. Another actress involved, Tamsin Greig (who I knew from the hilarious hospital-based comedy *Green Wing*), pointed out that these stories show that "there's wonder to be found in ordinary lives." Wonder and horror, I'd argue, as Bennett's dark side is on full display here with serial killing husbands, mothers in love with their sons, and park-attendant paedophiles. I wouldn't particularly call that ordinary, but maybe I've led a sheltered life.

In 2004, Bennett wrote his aformentioned *The History Boys*, a play adapted o film in 2006. The comedy drama follows a group of Sheffield grammar schoolboys preparing to get into Oxbridge with the help of a new, young teacher and self-proclaimed Oxbridge graduate. Cue coming of age frustrations, self-doubt, and sexual experimentation.

Reflecting on the phenomena of Northern writers, Bennett mused that they like to have it both ways in that they bang on about succeeding against the odds of their poverty, whilst insisting that Northern living is more honest than a cushty Southern life. I assume by 'they' he includes himself, also a Leeds lad who went to Oxford then spent the rest of his life living in London and writing about the North (among lots of other things). Though Geordie writer Jack Commons argued that such a separation from your roots is not always a choice: "The moment any of us shows a bit of social awareness or insight we at once make a gentleman of him, thus segregating him from his subject matter and compelling him to work by memory for the rest of his life."

Modern Northern writers who have bucked this trend include Huddersfield poet and author of *All Points North*, Simon Armitage, who was a former probation officer like his father but left the job to pursue writing full-time; a move that proved successful as he was appointed Poet Laureate in 2019 following his predecessor, Carol Ann Duffy. While in high school I learned Carol's Havisham and John Agard's *Half-Caste*, schoolkids today might learn Armitage's *Kid* or *Homecoming*. Armitage has also written books such as 2009 memoir *All Points North* as well as *Walking Home: Travels with a Troubadour on the Pennine Way* about his 2012 journey across the two-hundred-and-fifty-six miles of undulations running down the centre of the country. Whilst in lockdown in 2020, he also wrote a poem inspired by the boundary stone of Eyam in Yorkshire, when the village was quarantined in 1666. During the seventeenth century 'lockdown', two star-crossed lovers were forced apart until, Armitage imagines, the woman came no longer.

More recently, another Yorkshire poet, Wakefield's Ben Taylor, went viral after posting a video of himself walking through countryside reading his lockdown spoken word poem, written and performed – like all his work – in Tyke dialect:

The same folk that hashtags 'BeKind'
And now they're stockpiling bog roll and pasta,
And when t'government tell 'em stop home
Queue up in their hundreds down Asda.

He goes on to suggest a number of ways to stay busy when stuck between your four walls, adding:
Take up drawing like tha did as a bairn,

learn a language, write poems and words.
Mind, I could do without any more rivals,
so stay clear of dialect verse.

I did indeed heed his advice (this book is my lockdown baby), though I say the more the merrier on the dialect front.

I was not the only woman writing around that time as *The Guardian* reported that, as of 2021, 75 per cent of books in the general and literary fiction genre were by women. Gone are the days of writing under male pen names, the publishing industry is now dominated by women. From what I've heard of late (my reliable source here is Twitter), it's still very much a middle-class world, but one attempting to diversify in other ways, searching for stories from people of colour, writers with disabilities, and the queer community. Interestingly, I may have been one of the few women writing non-fiction, as books such as the travelogue remain the realm of men.

Do we think women may fail at reading their map, get lost, and have nothing to write about as they slink back home after a kindly gentleman has guided them back to the train station? Or do women simply prefer not to travel alone for fear of getting harassed along the way? A legitimate consideration, making inventing worlds from the safety of your kitchen a perhaps more attractive idea than having to tell yet another man on a train that you're married. When that doesn't work as he asks "well, where is he?", as if you should be surgically attached to your spouse, you get off a few stops earlier to escape, then you are a bit lost after all, and now there are other men staring at you in a new place, 'cos creepy men seem to be a planetary issue. I may or may not be speaking from experience here.

The publishing industry is also slowly moving away from London, with Northern indie publishers sprouting up in towns and cities from Hebden to Hull; with The Northern

Fiction Alliance linking them in a case of 'stronger together'. New Writing North is an organisation dedicated to developing Northern writers before they find their way to said publishers, and new initiatives like the Working Class Writers Festival set up in 2021 celebrates (it does what it says on the tin) working class writers from across the UK. As Wakefield writer, Richard Smyth, argues: "The North has always spoken in many voices", and moves like the ones mentioned above ensure that this continues to be the case.

At the beginning of this chapter, it was said that the North can be seen as a place of transformation. From the writers and publishers investing in local talent and damming the North-to-South brain drain, to the artistic creations to come out of it both reflecting and assisting in this evolution by pushing us to think, laugh, and cry with the characters so many of us know and love so well. In writing this chapter, I don't mean to create a new list that anyone feels they 'should' read; I still believe in reading whatever you enjoy most, regardless of who wrote it or what it's about. But I do think that people should know about writing and writers that they can see themselves in, that mirror their lives, or retell them in ways that make our understanding of our worlds just a little bit clearer.

X. What's on t' Telly?

"Choccie biccie?" I'm sat in my sister's house waiting for *Hollyoaks* to come on the telly as her fella makes his way through a packet of Digestives. "I can't believe this is still running. Or that you still watch it." I say, shaking my head in amazement.

"It's Chester, isn't it? Gotta support local," she explains. My sister's TV is usually off during the day, dictated by their young children until bedtime, then teatime is when the adults get a run of the box. Over at my retired parents' place, my dad's morning ritual involves turning on the telly and lowering himself into his chair, cup of tea in hand. After a day of pottering around the garden/garage (delete as weather appropriate), the TV is back on around four o'clock, tea replaced by a beer, the sound of a can opening meaning it's time for *A Place in the Sun*, followed by my mum's five o' clock *The Chase*. This ritual is completed by my parents bickering over what to watch after tea, usually ending with them putting on some questionably acted gangster film my dad has chosen.

Then I'm practically a Luddite, hauling around the same

TV I've had since the noughties when my teenage years consisted of unsuccessfully trying to see every film ever made (I'm more of a series binger now). What we can all agree on, however, is that the lounge furniture should be organised around being able to see the telly. And we're not alone.

Something that can unite North and South alike is that, as a nation, we watch more TV than we'd probably like to admit. Some argue this is due to a correlation between colder climates and increased viewing habits – I know I'd happily sit in a sunny plaza after work if that were an option. However, there are regional differences. According to Guerrillascope, in 2016 the Northeast led in the most hours watched per week at 34.7 hours, largely family-oriented, with Londoners the least at 27.6. Twenty-eight per cent of folks in the Northwest ate breakfast in front of the tube, though London led in TV dinners at 74 per cent of respondents.

But how did the small screen edge its way so resolutely into our lives? There are some who argue that the novelists' North is not the same as the North that people actually live in (see Richard Smyth's 2021 article 'How northern is the northern novel?'). While you may or may not agree, television has a down-to-earth appeal where it is not such a big leap to transport yourself from behind the lace curtains of your front room to whatever's happening on the other side of the screen.

History was made in 1888 when the first ever moving images were filmed in Leeds by Frenchman-turned-Leodiensian Louis Le Prince, who shot pictures of Roundhay Park and Leeds Bridge. Mysteriously, and not without conspiracy theories, on his way to share his invention with the world he disappeared without a trace before he could board a train to Paris. Regardless of his vanishing, thanks to Louis, art took a new form, stories could be enjoyed in action, and a new date idea was gifted to the lovers of the world.

During the height of the recent pandemic, it also came in handy when those of us not on the frontlines were relegated to our sofas to binge watch TV and wait for the world to end, or for those in charge to figure out how to save us. Instead of re-runs of *Friends* or *Buffy the Vampire Slayer*, I took it upon myself to watch anything Northern that previously escaped my viewing (or re-watch the classics). From this endeavour, I noticed that you could probably fit Northern TV and film somewhere on a coordinate plane.

The x axis would run from those works that play on and reinforce Northern stereotypes to those challenging them, with stuff that just happens to be set in the North positioned somewhere in the middle. The y axis would run from upper- to working-class North.

You could then plot where each series or movie would fall within these quadrants which, incidentally, I did one night when I couldn't sleep. As you might expect, there's a heavier concentration of things that fall into the stereotype/working-class quadrant, as Stuart Maconie pointed out, the idea of the North as "poor and primitive" holds fast in our national psyche, as can be seen on the page as well as the screen. "All of these contribute to the belief that the natural condition of the northerner is desperate near-destitution or at the very least a life spent watching the pennies."

Starting with a family-friendly creation that heavily evoked Northernness while dabbling across genres from action comedy to supernatural mystery, are stop-motion animation pair Wallace and Gromit. Against the backdrop of a mill town (possibly inspired by 1950s Wigan), their stories detail the various (mis)adventures of an eccentric homebody inventor and his anthropomorphic canine sidekick. In their 1989 short, *A Grand Day Out,* Wallace tells Gromit during take-off from the moon's surface, rocket shaking ominously: "Hold on lad, and think of Lancashire hotpot."

That said, Wallace's accent is from t'uther side of the Pennines and he's obsessed with Wensleydale cheese, a North Yorkshire creation. Southern actor Peter Sallis lends his unmistakable Yorkshire drawl to Wallace, while 2005's *The Curse of the Were-Rabbit* is helped along by the voices of Helena Bonham Carter and Peter Kay. Re-watching them during a time of global uncertainty, the weird and wonderful tales were reassuring. You always knew Wallace and Gromit would find their way safely home.

Another comforting show starring Sallis that drew on numerous stereotypes was *Last of the Summer Wine*. It ran from 1973-2010, making it the longest running situational comedy anywhere in the world. It is based on the simple and repetitious – but apparently popular – premise of a group of doddery old men pottering about a West Yorkshire village, mithering long-suffering, battleaxe women in hair curlers and baggy tights who tolerate their mishaps. Simon Armitage reckons it was originally minimalist and existential, so I re-watched the pilot episode. There was a scene where Cleggy is telling a priest how he saw a man carry a "quivering bird" across a road to then feed it to his cat. "Life is a complex mixture of competing moralities," he muses. The priest then asks for a fag since "it wouldn't be fitting for me to be seen wanting to live forever." Throw in some political satire and sly jokes about class divisions and I see what he means. The show is filmed in and around Holmfirth, bringing fame to the Yorkshire villages. Simon argued that, although people in the surrounding villages have gained being able to point out places they recognise on telly, shelves stocked with show paraphernalia instead of baked beans may be a trade-off worth contesting.

If we're talking longevity, then there is, of course, the iconic and ever-popular *Coronation Street*, the first soap opera to be set in the North. It first aired in 1960, reaching its gobsmacking ten thousandth episode on 7 February 2020 and there have been at least another 1,000 since, if my maths is up to scratch. The year I was born, a record-breaking twenty-six million viewers watched the Christmas Day episode to see hair-curler-wearing Hilda Ogden make her final appearance after twenty-three years on the show. My mate's younger sister has as a strong childhood memory of her duty shouting the '*Corrie* call' up the stairs to her family when the programme started "It's onnnnnn!" Her cousin gained serious brownie points when she grew up to direct some episodes. *Corrie is* also officially the UK's most popular soap. Allegedly, more people tuned in to watch Ken and Deirdre's wedding than did for Charles and Camilla's. It also featured British soap's first permanent transgender character, Hayley Cropper.

Set in a fictional town, based on Salford, the brick terraces seen in its opening credits – accompanied by mournful Northern band music – are of the type once ubiquitous in the area but which are now mostly gone from the town centre. A fans' tour was based in Manchester's Granada Studios in an attempt to create a 'Hollywood-on-the-Irwell', referring to the nearby river. It attracted over five million visitors but closed in 1999 as visitor numbers waned; I suppose once you've seen it, you don't need to go again. It briefly reopened in 2014, I guess to allow a new bunch of people to have their nosy about, closing again in 2015 as history repeated itself.

Another popular, long-running soap *Emmerdale Farm* – nowadays just *Emmerdale* – was launched in 1972. Set in a small Yorkshire village amid a perhaps disproprtionate number of rural scandals and full-on major disasters, it is Britain's third most popular soap after *EastEnders*, which launched in 1985. In 1982, Channel 4's Liverpool-based Brookside arrived which its creator, Phil Redman, intended to be an antidote to the "rose-tinted view of the plucky Northerner."

Not a massive fan of soaps, I did have to give *Hollyoaks* a go when it first came out in 1995 as it's set in my hometown and I wanted to see if I recognised any people or places. It had a younger, sexier cast than the other soaps, nicking a few *Corrie* actors in the process. I was disappointed to find out they filmed at Lime Pictures in Liverpool, only popping in to capture the river or a farm every now and then, and most actors sounded more Manc than Cestrian. I did, however, have my fifteen seconds of fame when they shot near a café by the river I worked at as a teenager. I tried to shine, or at least not trip over the plastic chair legs and scold a customer's face with hot tea. I can report that the show is not a realistic portrayal of life in my hometown though, as life in the city is pretty low-key, what with there being no regular kidnappings or murder. Abundant affairs and partner-swapping could well be the case, but I couldn't reliably comment.

I also grew up with *Byker Grove* on in the kitchen whilst my mum made tea. Set in the Northeast about a youth club, running from 1989 to 2000, it gave the country Ant & Dec (briefly known as pop stars PJ and Duncan), who are national treasures today. It was the first time I'd heard a Geordie accent and the first time a British drama had tackled the issue of 'coming out' in a 1994 episode. Two great moments, though the tabloids did kick off about the latter.

Leaving behind terraced streets, a new type of Northern TV series began to emerge in the late 1990s, with the likes of *Cold Feet* coming out in '97. Set around the affluent areas of Didsbury and Bowdon in Manchester, the show followed thirty-somethings navigating life at the turn of the millennium with a range of issues from a stay-at-home mum struggling to cope whilst the husband disapproves of getting a nanny, a couple trying to get pregnant though the longer it takes the more the woman gets obsessed and the guy gets fed up, and a single woman dating a string of frustrating losers who can't make their minds up about her. The show came briefly back from the dead in 2016 (unlike one of the characters).

Deciding a series set in Manchester was not such a bad idea, in 1999 *Queer as Folk* portrayed the city's gay scene and ran for eight seasons. I remember first coming across it as a pre-teen, channel flicking after nine pm and saw Aiden Gillen doing some guy in a shower, which was not only a first for me, but for British telly too. One of the main characters is a fifteen-year-old schoolboy which, at the time I didn't think much of, though it now seems a bit seedy that twenty-nine-year-old serial shagger Stuart knew it. That issue aside, it was radical and sexy at a time when the gay community were still recovering from being associated with HIV/AIDS and the show firmly reclaimed the word 'queer'. You also get to see Manchester's iconic Canal Street so while the South might have Brighton, we have the Rochdale Canal.

Our Friends in the North came out in 1996. It was set in Newcastle and starred Christopher Eccleston and a pre-Bond Daniel Craig (also a Cestrian, by the way). It comprises nine hour-long episodes following four teens into middle age with politics enmeshed throughout the storyline, painting a picture that things are not only grim Up North, but all across the country. A few dodgy Geordie accent attempts are painful to listen to at first, but you get used to it. Beginning in the 1960s, we see one protagonist, an activist student, returning from volunteering for the US civil rights movement to find bulldozers knocking down the slum houses in his hometown. The show portrays the Tories' rise to power and the accompanying miner's strikes. On canvassing the neighbourhood for the Labour Party, one man tells our young student: "I've told the other lot and I'll tell yous, yous can all bugger off... because you come round here every five year with promises like pie crust, and then we never see yous again 'til the next time ya want our vote." The show finale ended with Oasis song 'Don't Look Back in Anger', which is frustrating after everything they take you through, and yet somehow fitting.

We've also had a slew of programmes based around family life on various Northern council estates, led by 1986's sitcom *Bread*, set in Liverpool, followed in 1998 by the ironically named *The Royle Family*, set in Manchester. The latter is based on a telly-loving family with scenes taking place in the family's front room as they chat about not much at all on the settee while various people come in and out, including Nana who ends up in varying stages of consciousness in a bed behind them. "Have you 'ad your tea? What d'ya 'ave?" The show's writers, Caroline Aherne and Craig Cash, appear as dozy couple Denise and Dave and the theme song sets the tone with Oasis's 'Half The World Away' this time.

Then came *Shameless* in 2004, based on another Manc family headed by an alcoholic single father-of-six. The show depicts their escapes around the estate whilst exploring issues of poverty, sexuality, drug addiction, and mental health through dark comedy. Its Burnley-born writer Paul Abbott's own story is drama enough. One of nine kids, he was left with their father after their mother started a new relationship. His father left a couple of years later leaving them in the care of their pregnant seventeen-year-old sister, and at age thirteen he was raped and then attempted suicide. After being placed into a more stable working-class family he joined a writers' circle at school and later left the University of Manchester to write for the BBC after Alan Bennett blessed his work.

Both *The Royle Family* and *Shameless* have in common a somewhat useless (I'm told by others 'endearing') patriarch. Ricky Tomlinson's character sits on his own ample arse, flies open, and fat shames the neighbour every time she comes over. Frank Gallagher is physically abusive to his kids when hammered, bitching about how when their mum left he could've given them over to the council, but didn't, so they should be grateful. Both shows were taken across the pond and remade into *The Kennedys* and *Shameless US*. Unlike the latter, which was about a working-class family in Chicago, the former portraying a 'redneck' family, didn't take off as it didn't survive the pilot episode.

Two of *The Royle Family* actors, Ralf Little and Sheridan Smith, were snatched up for *Two Pints of Lager and a Packet of Crisps*, which ran from 2001-2011 set in Runcorn, Cheshire where the show's creator grew up. Runcorn, in Old English, means 'spacious bay'. This makes the place sound romantic but, being down the road from me, I can reliably inform you that it's not. Susan Nickson was eighteen when she dreamed up the programme based around the lives of a group of twenty-somethings, nicking a couple of *Hollyoaks* actors to make up the rest of the cast. It's like the British version of *Friends*, but instead of the bright lights of New York and Central Perk it's a run-down cargo port and The Archer pub.

The title of the pilot episode gives you a sense of the show's vibe – Fags, shags, and kebabs – and the humour isn't what I'd call politically correct now. Johnny and Gaz spend most evenings in the pub pondering life's philosophical questions such as: Who invented the pie? whilst Gaz scratches his balls and Johnny avoids finding work. The girls give as good as they get with feistiness and potty mouths. When Donna thinks she pregnant, Janet tells her to think of the benefits to which Donna grudgingly admits there is the love and pride. Janet clarifies she means child benefits. "A council house is just waiting for ya. And you even get an inside bog if you have twins." There was also a rogue musical episode parodying '00s music videos which sounds like it shouldn't work but, well, judge for yourself.

Continuing those down-to-earth vibes there is, of course,

Peter Kay. Say his name to any Northerner and elicit one of the following quotes: "Garlic? Bread?!"; "It's spittiiiiiin'"; or a re-enactment of the dad jog. As well as his stand-up comedy, he responsible for *Phoenix Nights*, a 2001 sitcom co-written and starring Kay and the two other writers, Dave Spikey and Neil Fitzmaurice. The sitcom is about a working men's club in Bolton hosting bingo nights and mediocre stage acts. *Car Share* is Kay's most recent brainchild, premised on two friends, male and female, chatting as they drive to work through Greater Manchester. Kay's former real life Salford University mate Sian Gibson plays the passenger. I love how normal and Northern the chat is, but had to be convinced to watch it again by my mum, who giggles throughout each episode, after the first one I saw involved them making themselves feel better by slagging off their colleagues (who needs to watch a programme for that?).

During the first lockdown, I got stuck at my parents' for longer than the few weeks I thought it'd be. After I'd walked out of the umpteenth US gangster movie (they only have one telly), something we could all agree on watching were British police dramas. Compared with the former, there's something to be said for the lack of guns, instead watching coppers knock on doors and chase bad guys with only their wits to rely on. And it seems that crime dramas have not been this popular since Arthur Conan Doyle and Agathie Christie gifted us their novels in the late nineteenth and early twentieth century. According to evolutionary psychologists, we're drawn to such stories to stay vigilant to 'who', 'what', 'when', and 'where' of murder, rape, and theft so we can avoid the same befalling us and our loved ones.

There have been many great crime dramas set in the North, such as 2006's *Life on Mars*, based in noughties Manchester about a policeman (John Simm) who has a car accident and wakes up in the 1970s. He is condemned to solve crimes with his new police team, a smoke-filled, rule-breaking macho lot led by DCI Gene Hunt (Philip Glenister), while we wait to see if he wakes up in the right decade. And since it's the '70s there are some obligatory factory closure scuffles along the way, as well as great Northern utterances like "he 'ad breath that could strip the fur off a badger." The series also has a banging soundtrack with the show named after a David Bowie song staying faithful to the lyrics about a lawman beating up the wrong guy. A spin-off series *Ashes to Ashes* (another Bowie song) followed in 2008, this time with a female police officer (Keeley Hawes) in London with the same cops suffering her own trauma-based time travel.

Crime dramas where the communities are just as much of a character as the families in them, include 2019's *The Bay*, following a female officer navigate an investigation and her own entangled personal life in Morecambe, and 2024's *The Jetty*, also set in Lancashire around a female detective uncovering various crimes in her hometown that lead her back to her own family. As she unveils the misogyny that permeates her town, she begins to see the wood, not just the trees. To paraphrase Jeanette Winterson, there are women, men, and beasts, and it's not always easy to tell the latter two apart before it's too late.

But my favourite show with a kick-arse female police officer was 2014's *Happy Valley*. When I was in the US and the pandemic was largely a faraway issue, I was nevertheless told I could take time off when I came down with something flu-like. I was feeling a bit homesick and decided to find a Northern series to watch to blanket myself in familiar accents. I stumbled across the programme filmed in the Calder Valley, West Yorkshire, and can report that the valley was far from happy. The lead actress is the formidable Sarah Lancashire, and I couldn't tell if I was sweating from the fever or the drama. Despite all the crime, the dialect, community, and dark humour scratched an itch I had for home. Locals chatting at the corner shop juxtaposed with the flat blocks filled with "scrotes and smackheads", as our articulate protagonist put it. The backdrop reminded me of the Beatles' lyric about four thousand holes in Blackburn, Lancashire. Huddersfield's Sally Wainwright is the programme's writer and she is also responsible for the earlier *Last Tango in Halifax* from 2012 which, despite its title, is not quite as raunchy as the Paris version from which it takes its name. That show portrays two widowed singles who'd fancied each other in their youth though life had had other plans. The man and woman set out to rekindle their affections across class divides while their children splutter about in the background.

Wainwright is apparently a fan of actress Lancashire who appears here too, this time as a well-to-do headmistress having an affair with one of her female teachers. Wainwright explained her writing of such roles for women: "I find women more interesting. They seem more heroic. Women seem to have more to deal with...", evoking the notion of the 'triple shift'. Coined in 1995 by British sociologists Duncombe and Marsden, the term described how women are often saddled with not only a double shift of paid work and housework, but also the emotional labour of caring for the family – something that became starkly clear during women's attempts to work from home during the pandemic.

In 2019, Wainwright also adapted the story of Anne Lister into the TV series *Gentleman Jack*, concerning a woman in West Yorkshire during the Industrial Revolution in 1832. Meanwhile, Anne was waging her own revolution defying gender norms and searching for a wife, eventually marrying in the first known lesbian wedding. Details of her life were uncovered through her meticulous diaries which Wainwright used to, once again, create complex and exciting female characters. Expecting to love the woman for waging her way in a man's world, I found her at first embodying all the things I don't like about toxic masculinity – speaking down to those she managed, preying on younger women – but it turned out the tenant she argued with was a drunk abuser and the younger woman had been in love with her for years anyway. I warmed to her, admiring her gumption and intellect as she navigated life as a woman in the nineteenth century. As she declares in the portrayal that nature played a cruel trick on her "putting such a bold spirit in this vessel." It was said that Miss Lister frequently visited the Ladies of Llangollen, two well-to-do women who co-habited instead of marrying, denying accusations of lesbianism.

Another popular period drama was 2010's *Downton Abbey* which ran for six seasons and, in 2019, spawned a film. Set at the beginning of the twentieth century, the show depicts a fictional country estate in Yorkshire, documenting societal changes as seen from the perspective of both the servants and the masters. In this upstairs/downstairs set up, my family would have fallen into the latter category, as my great aunt Alice was a live-in housekeeper of Chatterton Hey, a mill owner's home in Bury. When the owners died, they left money for my aunt and uncle to buy a terraced house, and the estate became a residential home for men with substance misuse disorder.

As with Wainwright, though firmly in the world of comedy, another woman writing interesting characters for women was Victoria Wood. She wrote and starred in *Dinnerladies* (1998-2000), a sitcom set in a fictional factory canteen in Manchester, also starring Julie Walters and a host of other Northern women with cracking comic timing. Victoria, a Lancashire lass with an observational eye for Northern culture and for satirising class in her sketches, plays, films and sitcoms, once observed that life wasn't fair as "some of us drink champagne in the fast lane, and some of us eat our sandwiches by the loose chippings on the A597". Julie said of her work with Victoria: "Oh, all the time when Victoria Wood and I did our series, people were asking, 'Can women be funny?' People still ask that? It's like asking: 'Can women breathe in and out?'" Research from 2023 showed what I already suspected: that Northern women are the funniest people in Britain. While Northern men may be the most popular comics, when 2,000 Brits were asked where their funniest friend came from, Northern women came top.

There are other offerings I know I've missed, but these examples show a range of contributions that have kept us laughing and crying over the years. From the political or the naff to the melodramatic and the hilarious, we've reproduced and challenged stereotypes, and shown life at its exceptional and mundane on the small screen and big screen too.

Countless films have portrayed or emerged from the North. I've already mentioned some literature transformed for the box, so here I mention original productions that challenged the popularity of adaptations.

Voted one of the top ten greatest films ever made after its release, 1945's *Brief Encounter*, whilst not about the North, was filmed in Carnforth train station. The famous romance is a story of two married strangers' chance encounter that ends in heartbreak when they must end their love affair when the doctor goes to South Africa. In a similar vein, my grandma met her future husband at that very same station, leading to them writing to each other when apart (though he was only in Reading, a fair bit closer than Africa).

But beginning with more modern stories set in the North, there are a range of productions portraying the decline of the North's industry and its aftermath. For example, there's the 1996 film *Brassed Off*. Marketed somewhat bizarrely as a romantic comedy in the US, it's firmly about the devastation that the mine closures wreaked in one Yorkshire town. Ewan McGregor does have a love interest, but I'd hardly call it a romcom. The film follows the story of a colliery brass band and their struggles in and out of the mine, two exemplary Northern cultural relics. There's in-fighting between the miners, bailiffs taking away family furniture, a guy in hospital "coughing up coal", and a clown (in the literal red-nose-big-shoes sense) that tries to hang himself. It's loosely based on the journey of the Grimethorpe Colliery Band who did indeed win first place at the Albert Hall. Warrington's Pete Postlethwaite delivered a rousing speech at the finale when he said that music mattered, but "not compared to how people matter... Over the last ten years this bloody government has systematically destroyed an entire industry... our communities, our homes, our lives. All in the name of progress and for a few lousy bob."

Also set in a mining town against the backdrop of strikes, this time in County Durham, is *Billy Elliot*, a dance drama from 2000. In a reversal of the usual series of events, the film was later made into a book by Melvin Burgess, as well as a musical. The film was inspired by the real story of a – now international – opera singing boy from the Northeast. The film stars Julie Walters as the no-nonsense dance teacher secretly supporting Billy. When she offers him free private dance classes, he asks if she fancies him, to which she replies: "Funnily enough, Billy, I don't. Now piss off." I also distinctly remember the scene where Billy is with a classmate who suddenly offers to show him her fanny. If memory serves, he politely declines. Sweet Northern romance.

In a similar vein, *The Full Monty* is a 1997 comedy about a group of men dealing with unemployment due to the steel factory closures in Sheffield. Despite the gritty and very real back story – we meet one sorry character trying to gas himself in his car – the film manages to be silly and touching, falling firmly into the British favourites category and immortalising the post office dance scene to Donna Summer's 'Hot Stuff'.

A less light-hearted look at being on the dole came from the utterly depressing film *I, Daniel Blake*. I saw it while living in Madrid and came out wondering what had happened to my country's famed social support in the years I'd been away. Ken Loach's 2016 film portrays a widowed carpenter in Newcastle who turns to the welfare system after a heart attack renders him unable to work. What follows is a tragic story of the system failing someone in genuine need, a story that is sadly not an anomaly in Britain after years of austerity and weeding out of the feared 'benefit scrounging'.

Moving away from largely white working-class northern communities, *White Girl* was a 2008 drama about a single mum's move from a Leeds flat to a terraced house in a predominantly Muslim neighbourhood in Bradford. Her daughter, the white girl in question, finds in Islam a safe haven from the chaos in her house as her mum (Anna Maxwell Martin) struggles with alcohol and an aggressive on-again-off-again drug-pushing fella. In a film with a very different approach to viewing the multicultural North, Islamic extremism was explored, tongue firmly in cheek, in the 2010 black comedy *Four Lions*, written by satirist Chris Morris. The film follows a group of incompetent British jihadis attempting to carry out an attack in Sheffield. Not your typical comedy topic, but if being able to poke fun at anything and everything isn't British, I'm not sure what is.

As I was reminiscing about these films, I realised again that most of them couldn't pass the Bechdel test which requires movies to (1) have at least two women in it who (2) talk to each other about something other a man. I suppose *The Full Monty* does discuss mental health and body issues that men also face, which is often not discussed in life, let alone in art, but I was hoping to find a Northern *Made in*

Dagenham or *Bend It Like Beckham*. Scouse actress Rita Tushingham, star of 1960s kitchen sink classic *A Taste of Honey*, says the one regret of her long career is that her directorial debut, *Victory Girls*, hasn't yet been made. The film is about a group of women working in a First World War ammunitions factory in Preston and I eagerly await its manifestation.

Of the few films I have found about women, 2004's *School for Seduction* didn't exactly scream feminism. An Italian woman played by Kelly Brook moves from Naples to Newcastle to teach women (and a drag queen) how to tantalise men, arguing that women shouldn't have to choose between being feminine or feminist: "It's not about pleasing men, it's about pleasing yourself." This was, however, followed by lessons in how to stroke a broom seductively and suggestively fondle sausages in the chippy. The film did touch on some more serious issues though, like that of a single mother working two jobs trying to get a promotion whilst battling a male boss who stole her ideas and told her to "stick to the register". Another woman's husband resented her career success and told her to quit her job, complaining he wanted a real wife, not one that spouts off about their managerial problems. So a bit of a mixed bag.

A serious contender for passing the test is a favourite of mine, the feel-good *Calendar Girls*. The 2003 production is about a bunch of Yorkshire village Women's Institute ladies who get their wobbly bits out for a WI calendar to raise money for cancer research in honour of a member who lost her husband. Julie Walters is joined by Helen Mirren, as well as Yorkshire's Penelope Winton. Despite the film centring around them getting their kit off, I reckon it would pass the test with flying colours (not just flying bras).

In terms of the thespians behind these interpretations, some names crop up consistently. Though we seem to cast

Julie Walters in everything Northern (and she reunited with Jamie Bell in 2019's *Film Stars Don't Die in Liverpool*) she's actually a Brummie. Despite this, I reckon we could make her an honorary Northern, and not just because Birmingham is seen by some as the North, but because she grew up working-class so can relate to the roles. She actually joined a number of actors calling out the lack of opportunity for working-class kids to get into acting nowadays,. If she were starting her career in modern times, she reckons she wouldn't have got anywhere. Walters is one of Britain's best-loved actresses, winning a whole host of BAFTAs, sharing first place with Dame Judi Dench for being nominated for the most awards.

Dame Judi is from Heworth, near York, though for the longest time I didn't know that because she certainly rocks the King's English. Another actor I initially had no idea was Northern – even after I saw him leading the floats at Manchester's Pride parade – is Sir Ian McKellen. He's actually from Burnley, twenty miles down the road. His best mate, Patrick Stewart is also a Northerner, from Huddersfield, though that one got past me too (they are known for setting great bromance goals and McKellen even married Stewart and his wife). It must be all that time at the Royal Shakespeare Company with Ian and Judi. I did, however, come across Stewart recounting a poem in Yorkshire dialect that his auntie used to recite every Christmas:

I was sittin' be our'sen th' last e'ening,
Me mother n' father were off
'Cause they'd 'eard me ol' aunt Susannah
were laid up in bed wi' a cough.
She's some brass, me ol' aunt Susannah,
'At's the reason she's looked after so;
If they've nowt, well, they're nowt but a bother.
There's a samp'un, me ol' uncle Joe.

'Samp'un' was an expression that left me stumped, though perhaps we could ask Sean Bean (who is definitely Northern). Sheffield-born Bean was studying welding when he happened across an art class, giving us *Lady's Chatterley's Lover* of D.H. Lawrence fame, Sergeant Sharpe (a favourite of my mum's), ring-protecting Boromir, and *Game of Thrones's* Ned Stark. I stopped watching the latter when they (spoiler alert) impaled his head on a stick. He can now be heard doing voiceovers for various adverts, including the county's eponymous tea.

Another actress proudly displaying her Northern accent was the thirteenth *Doctor Who*. It was controversial enough when they cast a woman but, to add insult to injury, she came from Skelmanthorpe. Jodie Whittaker said she was "lucky" she could keep her own accent which, in 2018, is quite telling. Amusingly, when I was watching an interview on a US chat show, the subtitles informed us she was from "Hoodezfield" writing her hometown as they phonetically heard it. Now that I think about it, the first Doctor in the remake was Salfordian Christopher Eccleston, though they felt the need to address his accent in the first episode when teen singer-turned-actress Billie Piper asked him why he sounded like he was from the North. "All planets have a North," he replied.

Then there's one actress famous for hiding her accent, Dame Patricia Routledge of sitcom *Keeping Up Appearances* fame. Originally from the Wirral, she played Hyacinth Bucket ("pronounced 'bouquet'") from 1990-1995, though I still see replays in both the UK and US. Her clipped tones conceal her humble beginnings, while the rest of her family threaten to reveal her working-class background with their 'common' accents and conduct. The enduring popularity of this show is not only her knack for physical comedy, but the relatability of the protagonist, as most people know someone with Hyacinth-like qualities, straining to climb the social ladder in Britain's class-based society.

Looking back at what is only a slice of a vast and varied pie, Northern TV, film, and thespians have shown us what it means to be from or inhabit a place: to be shaped by it and mould it with new ideas and people and progress. To be explorers of secret gardens, the Islamic faith, or cheese-y moons. To write love letters to a landscape, to scream to escape a city's oppressive streets, or to struggle to preserve a community in the face of a rapidly changing world.

Television has not only entertained us but educated us by transporting us through history or reflecting our reality back in ways that can be uplifting or a punch us in the gut.

Or both, as is often the case.

XI. The North Will Rise Again

Aged fifteen, my band and I rehearsed in the rock-n-roll location of my parents' garage in our otherwise quiet village. Luckily, my next-door neighbour was more than supportive of our racket, being an AC/DC fan himself. My hair was cut short and bleached blonde apart from a black fringe, which I thought was the height of cool at the time, modelling my look on the lead singers of pop punk bands who were mostly male. Looking back at photos, I looked more like Sonic the Hedgehog, if Sonic had worn stripy socks on his arms and baggy Soho's that were ripped from trailing through puddles in torn Converse.

But my music taste (and fashion sense) was not always so grungy. According to my mother, when I emerged flailing into the world a week early, she'd been listening to Kate Bush on repeat for months. Because of this, I never got to hear a song released that year by Scouse band The Icicle Works called 'Up Here in the North of England', which included lyrics about McDonald's finally finding us and Southerners not liking us. The first music I can remember being obsessed with was a mix of Michael Jackson's *Bad*, Bryan Adams's *Waking Up the Neighbours* (another of mum's favourites), and Alanis Morissette's *Jagged Little Pill*, which remains one of my favourite albums. An American and two Canadians. The arrival of the Spice Girls into my pre-teen years, with their two Northern Mels, not only extended my feminist education – albeit in a different vein to Alanis – but also heralded the start of my listening to more British music. Next came other girl bands rocking great harmonies like Eternal and All Saints, as well as boy bands Take That (Gary Barlow is from Cheshire and Mark is from Oldham) and Ireland's Boyzone. Then came the Brit Pop bands, Blur, Pulp, and Oasis, as well as Wales's Stereophonics (who I only got into after my friend bribed me with her CD to convince me to let her watch *Big Brother* at a sleepover).

Oasis is a quintessentially Northern group, principally made up of Mancunian brothers Liam and Noel Gallagher. The first song I learned on the guitar was 'Wonderwall', every busker's crowd-pleaser. My sister, Clare, lived in Manchester for a few years and thus began her love affair with the city's music scene. One day she had just left home when she received a message from her housemate ordering her to get The Red Lion pub because Liam Gallagher was there. She obviously ditched what she was doing, did a U-turn, and headed straight over. Turns out it was a wake, but that didn't stop a throng of admirers going to talk to him. Apparently, he didn't seem to mind, so she approached. Contrary to his infamous grumpy persona, Clare says he was very friendly. My sister remembers saying something lame like "I love you and have your poster on my wall" to which she tells me he replied, "nice one" or 'something Manchester like that'. So true is her love for Oasis that my niece is named after one of their songs. Incidentally, Liam's full name is William John Paul Gallagher, a tribute to the Beatles, and he also named one of his kids Lennon, so my sis is not the only one paying tribute to her musical heroes.

When I asked Clare about her experience living in Manchester, she replied that people from Manchester love Manchester. They wax lyrical about the city and, as long as you are a willing candidate to join the cult, they'll love you too. She insists that one of the binding agents of Mancunians is the music. The aptly-named website, ilovemanchester.com, proudly reports the city is crowned the rock and indie capital of the UK. There is, of course, the legendary Factory Records music label representing bands such as James, Joy Division who later morphed into New Order, and Happy Mondays. Not to mention the Haçienda night club which cradled the rave scene of the 1990s. The above earned the city the nickname 'Madchester'. The latter drug-fuelled era was dramatised in Michael Winterbottom's 2002's film, *24 Hour Party People*, which ended with the sombre reflection that when the come-downs are worse than the come-ups are fun, it's time to rein it in. And rein it in they did on screen, as well as in real life where the rave scene waned (at least until lockdown made everyone stir crazy and six thousand Mancunians met for an illegal rave resulting in three people stabbed, one woman raped, and one guy dying of an overdose).

A testament to the lighter side of Manchester's madness is the multi-floored indoor market Afflecks Palace, which used to be a drapery business selling fabrics and furs that is now, in their words, "an emporium of eclecticism, a totem of indie commerce". Some call it the Camden Market of the North. I used to go there as a teenager to buy band badges for my school bag and ogle the neon sex toys. Another popular item is anything with "AND ON THE SIXTH DAY GOD CREATED MANCHESTER" printed on it.

With the Haçienda long gone by the time my sister got there in 2009, she instead frequented the weekly indie nights where she wistfully recalls being able to go out wearing anything you wanted, unlike other places where you have to get dressed up. Face animated, she told me how the last song of the night would often be the Stone Roses's 'I am the Resurrection', causing everyone to 'go mental', singing and hugging each other.

That said, it's not only elated embracing that Manchester inspires. Minus Rick Astley's 2023 Glastonbury tribute (that was inexplicable gold), am I the only one who finds The Smiths depressing? Apparently not, since the *Manchester Evening News* reported that, after an analysis of lyrics, only 5.2 per cent of the songs could be deemed 'happy'. Songs such as 'Unhappy Birthday' and 'Girlfriend in a Coma' scored 90 per cent on their misery scale, helping win them the accolade of "one of the most miserable bands ever". Despite this, many argue the band changed their lives, with music-lover and Smiths fan Stuart Maconie claiming that while Thatcher "witchlike, cast the north into the outer darkness, The Smiths' songs illuminated it anew with northern lights and fireworks." Though with lyrics about rain falling on humdrum towns that drag people down, I wonder if the light actually came from bored teens who'd set fire to a wheelie bin.

The mate of mine who moved from Chester to Liverpool (which she loved), then Manchester (which she didn't), and is now happily in Whitley Bay, said she finds Manchester too cliquey. You're either part of the gay scene or the dance scene or the indie scene. My sister fell comfortably into the latter, so I guess you have to choose your Manc cult wisely, hope they let you in, and then if they do, you're stuck with that. Funnily enough, recently I stumbled across two other instances of people lacking appreciation for the Northwestern city. One was on a postcard gifted to a friend in Leeds, who is from Manchester, which read: "Leeds. At least it's not Manchester". The second came from the book *Good Omens* by Terry Pratchett and Neil Gaiman, which explains how demons had created value-added tax, and Manchester. Which I thought was a bit harsh.

Despite this Manchester curiosity, at least when I was a teenager, anywhere was more exciting than Chester so I would sneak out at any chance I got. Lucky for me, the UK only cracked down on IDs when I turned eighteen, so I ventured far and wide to get my kicks, at least Manchester and Liverpool felt intrepid back then. Sometimes we would cross the border into Wales to attend a crummy rock night called, if I remember correctly, Unchained. I once tried to check out Sheffield's music scene as my mate's brother's band was playing and one of us had just passed our driving test. The infamous 'Snake Pass' had other plans, however, as the road was flooded so that was that plan thwarted. Another favourite place of mine to sneak off to was Liverpool to go to the Krazyhouse with its three floors of rock music. Nights of jumping about in the mosh pit, getting a snog in at the end of the night, then staying awake until six am – just us and the pigeons of Lime Street Station – waiting to get the first train home. The alternative was getting the last train home which meant you missed half the night and had to return with beer cans and vomit rolling towards your feet every time the train rounded a corner.

Liverpool can, and historically has, rivalled Manchester for the title of rock capital of Britain. I don't need to tell you it was the birthplace of The Beatles. The working-class boys in suits contrasted with London's private school good-boys-gone-bad The Rolling Stones. While the Stones imitated the Southern drawl of the USA, the Beatles' Scouse accent peeked through when they sang, arguably making it fashionable to be Northern. I also don't need to tell you about how they revolutionised pop music and brought out the fanaticism in the word 'fans' with Beatlemania. After the Beatles went their separate ways, George Harrison had a hit in 1971 with 'My Sweet Lord', revering the Hindu god Krishna, while later that year John Lennon released 'Imagine' in which he asks people to envisage a world without religion. So maybe their spiritual differences contributed to their fall out and it wasn't Yoko after all. Lennon and Ono moved to New York to escape British tabloids' racist and sexist scrutiny, going on to write political music including 'Woman is the N----- of the World', inspired by an Irish revolutionary who argued that women workers are the slave of the slave. Perhaps unsurprisingly, some critics questioned their controversial use of the N word, and many radio stations refused to play it due to their use of the word at all.

You can of course take the Beatles tour of Liverpool which, as well as taking you past Penny Lane and Strawberry Fields, will show you the fabled Cavern Club, the underground bar that launched their career – and hosted them 275 times – as well as having many other stars grace the stage with their presence. I took my Brazilian ex there one year as he loved British rock music and he shed a tear (though, to be fair, he had sunk a few pints). He was later astonished to see that everybody in the pub we entered afterwards was pissed at nine pm, belting out classics at the karaoke night. "It's like Sao Paulo at two am," he declared part amused, part horrified. Welcome to Liverpool.

There is also the lesser known, first ever female rock band who also came out of Liverpool in 1963, The Liverbirds. Named after the iconic statues atop the Liver building on the docks and a cute play on words, as much as I dislike women being called 'birds' or 'chicks'. Hailed the female Beatles, their time in the sun waned five years later as gendered duties of marriage and motherhood called. The 1980s Liverpool post-punk scene also attracted a seventeen-year-old Courtney Love, US rocker and lover of the deceased Nirvana frontman,

Kurt Cobain, who had previously been living in a Dublin squat. Of the experience, Love has said: "Before Liverpool my life doesn't count... Liverpool had been a great school to become a rock star."

Merseyside has since continued to inspire and churn out decent bands such as The Coral and The Zutons. If I had to choose a favourite song though, I'd go with Space's 'Beautiful Neighbourhood'. After describing a host of colourful characters on their street including a transvestite and a murderous priest, they defy any bulldozers that want to knock down their 'hood for thinking they're "scum". Classic Scouse attitude. Speaking of which, the mate I mentioned before who preferred Liverpool over Manchester warned me that "Manchester is Northern but Liverpool is just Scouse." Though Liverpool is often credited with being more international than Manchester due to its US-facing seaport, Manchester's Twisted Wheel and Wigan Casino dance halls are testament to the growth of the peculiar emergence of the Northern Soul movement of the 1960s. The movement was inspired by American soul and R'n'B, emulating Motown records; a way to refuse to listen to music made in London, with one Casino-goer in *The Sunday Times* heralding the end of "all of them southerners telling us what to do." Or, telling us we're shit as acid house band The KLF did in their 1990 bizarre club song 'It's Grim Up North', which simply lists a bunch of towns and cities, many of which aren't grim at all.

Unlike Manchester with its live music in every other pub, Chester has less to offer as, growing up, we only had jazz bar, Alexander's, and the Marlborough Arms, affectionately called 'The Marlb' and spelled 'Marlbororough' after a ghost scared the guy working on the sign. It's an old man pub popular with service staff after their shifts, where I've done a couple of open mic nights and my mate's band used to practice in the attic. The former also has a great weekly open mic night which used to display the talents of Welsh singer Duffy before her rise to fame, as well as yours truly (I'm still waiting for my record deal). The long-time hosts of this night make up an integral part of the club, a local folk band led by a jolly bearded man with an uncanny likeness to Father Christmas.

Music has long been praised for exploring meaning in our messy human lives, getting us through tough times, and bringing people together to celebrate good ones. When I lived in Leeds, I spent much of my time in the city's music venues listening to the range of genres on offer from dubstep to soul.

The Brudenell Social Club, frequented by students and locals alike, has long been a staple of the local music scene. I remember going there with a guy I was seeing and realised that the old man wallpaper matched my date's old man jumper. I think it was an ironic fashion statement, but we didn't date too much longer for me to find out. I also loved an old warehouse which had been converted into a space for live music and hosted a wicked roast dinner and jazz day on Sundays. It was pretty chilly in there but, on request, the owner would ascend the metal staircase and return offering furry, musty blankets from what I gather was his own living space. The former stands resolute in its musical offerings, though the latter is no longer there.

As well as smaller music venues, Britain's summer festivals are long-awaited with thousands assembling to enjoy them, come mud or sunburn. One of the oldest music festivals still in existence, the Reading Festival, began in 1961 as the National Jazz and Blues Festival, later morphing into rock and recruiting Leeds to offer Northern music-lovers a closer event. I went to the latter as a fourteen-year-old and never went again. I lost my friends during Blink 182 trying to get to the front, got kicked in the back of head by a crowd surfer, had a panic attack and had to be pulled out of the mosh pit by bouncers. Sadly, the paramedics would not let me watch the rest of the show from backstage once I'd stopped snuffling into a paper bag. Later, I didn't sleep a wink as different camps, blatantly off their faces, were shouting to each other "cabbage!" "lettuce!" all night. In the morning, I woke up to a stale loaf of bread being lobbed at my head and to the news that someone had died from a drug-related accident. Since then, I have stuck to family-friendly festivals. For instance, ten years later when I was living in Leeds doing a master's, some friends and I decided to go to the Filey Folk Festival to get some sea air and music therapy. We rented a big, old, peeling house on the beachfront and wandered around the town catching street acts and pub performances. Great music, great company, great sleep, and no-one died.

Yorkshire has produced a couple of well-known folk songs, 'Scarborough Fair' being one, sang about a medieval event no longer occurring, though replaced by a museum collection of fairground rides. Another in dialect that you may have had sung at you by a proud Yorkie is 'On Ilkley Moor Baht' At'. I told my parents one day when they were round for tea that I only knew the chorus, at which point they both sprang into action, unprompted. Like a car crash you can't look away from, they sang all verses in their entirety. I lost track in amusement after the ducks came to eat up the worms. Turns out what sounded to my ears like 'by tat' actually means 'without hat' and the worms came to eat you because you didn't wrap up warm like your mam probably warned you to. Incidentally, Ilkley Moor is also responsible for Yorkshire's biggest boulder, the Hitching Stone, flung north-westerly by a witch who reportedly resented it for spoiling her view. So, as well as the weather, flying rocks could also kill you.

From folk to pop, in more recent times, Yorkshire (Sheffield, to be precise) has birthed two famous Cockers: Joe whose gravelly voice got famous covering The Beatles's 'With a Little Help from My Friends' and Jarvis from Sheffield band Pulp. I told you about the American man who'd enjoyed Manchester because he'd met blue-collar workers: it reminded me of the lyrics from Pulp's popular song, 'Common People', about resenting tourists who enjoy 'slumming it' on vacation but wash off the chip grease once they've gone home. Since the two Cockers, the steel city has continued to provide with the Arctic Monkeys who were music to many people's ears as they didn't sing in an American-tinged accent. They called their debut album *Whatever People Say I Am, That's What I'm Not*, quoting a line from 1958 novel turned 1960 film *Saturday Night and Sunday Morning* about a rebellious man, partying and adultering his way across Nottingham. On that 2006 album they had a song called 'Mardy Bum' which, in my opinion, is a great title and a great song. Though I do remember ripping the CD player out of the wall after my drunken sister had played the disc on repeat for the fourth time in a row at a house party.

Along with the Arctic Monkeys, in 2005 came Newcastle's Maximo Park who similarly sang Northern and proud, as well as Leeds's Kaiser Chiefs who burst onto the charts with their 2004 romper 'I Predict a Riot', as well as Sunderland's The Futureheads' popular cover of Kate Bush's 'Hound of Love' released that same year. Most of my teenage years involved going to as many gigs as I could manage, and that included seeing the Kaiser Chiefs at Elland Road Stadium in Leeds in 2009. Other gigs I made it to included Manc band Elbow and Sussex's The Cure at the Old Trafford cricket ground in 2004 and Bryan Adams at the MEN arena in 2010. The MEN is now sadly known as the site of the horrific bombing in 2017 at an Ariana Grande concert, attended mostly by teenage girls, where twenty-three people died and hundreds were injured. Afterwards, the city rallied together and its symbol, the bee, could be seen everywhere in solidarity with those who had lost their lives. The bee, which represents Manchester's workers, was brought back into the limelight during the pandemic, with murals of the insect everywhere accompanied by writing such as 'Keep smiling, our kid'.

To the Northeast, the Police's Sting is from Tyne and Wear, though I think he's firmly a man of the world now with homes in London, New York, Malibu, Tuscany, and Wiltshire. When living in the US, I remembered the lyrics about drinking tea rather than coffee in 'Englishman in New York' when I was at a friend's house who had the biggest coffee machine but, when I asked for some tea, popped a cup of water in the microwave. Some cultural differences are small but cut deep. Sting returned to his hometown of Wallsend (named due to being where Hadrian's Wall ended in the east) in his 2014 musical *The Last Ship*, inspired by his upbringing near the local shipbuilding industry. The Tyne also provided musical inspiration when, two years after Roy Orbison had sat on the dock of the 'Frisco bay, Roger Whittaker sat on the banks of the River Tyne leaving 'Durham Town'. Though oceans apart, both are melancholic songs; something about bodies of water that make people introspective. More modern music coming out of this neck of the woods includes 'Geordie Bruce Springsteen' Sam Fender, a product of North Shields, who hit the charts with discerning songs like 'Seventeen Going Under' and 'The Borders' with themes of troubled adolescence and working-class frustration with political alienation. My mate says she sees him drinking in the pub every now and then, though he apparently struggles with being "that guy" in his small town. Despite this, he's claimed "you can take a lad out of Shields, but you can't take Shields out the lad."

The rock band I was in during my teen years had me on guitar and backing vocals, two other studded-belt-wearing women on bass and lead vocals, and a male drummer we'd pinched from another band. Despite the fact that the music which inspired our angsty thrashing was mostly male dominated, we looked to the models of Brody Armstrong (nowadays Brody Dalle), Courtney Love, Debbie Harry and Gwen Stefani, and had a go of it. Men seemed to have a monopoly on Northern rock music, with the exception of those oft-forgotten Liverbirds. Whilst there is no shortage of amateur female bands, few have achieved mainstream success like their manly counterparts. One pub in Middlesborough banned female-led groups from playing at the live music venue in 2017 after customers said they shouldn't be singing 'male songs'. The pub manager, herself a woman, reported: "I've been told that some women can sing and some can't, but they can't sing heavy rock."

Leeds's sweet-toned singer-songwriter Corinne Bailey Rae claims rock influences, but sings more soulful pop. Of her mixed-race heritage, she said she disliked being asked to choose 'white' or 'black' music, citing artists like Otis Redding and Jimi Hendrix as well as Led Zeppelin and Kurt Cobain as influences, the common thread being able to bare their souls in their art. Her debut song 'Put Your Records On' makes many top summer tunes list, mine included. Sadly, after her husband died of an accidental overdose in 2008, she claimed she'd never be able to write such breezy music again.

So where were all the women singing rock? Where were the female Def Leppards? County Durham punk band Penetration had a female singer in the 1970s; Sunderland DJ Lauren Laverne had a brief stint in pop-punk band Kenickie in the '90s; and Mel C did have a something of a rock phase – including a duet with Bryan Adams – but I drew a blank after this. What is it about quintessentially gritty rock that Northern women's voices haven't had access to? Female-led bands across our Atlantic archipelago such as Texas, The Cranberries, or Blondie would suggest that Northerners missed a trick here. And North America would certainly argue in favour with the likes of Tina Turner, Janis Joplin, Joan Jett, and Alanis Morissette scratching out gravely rocking classics. But, as Little Mix's South Shields member Jade Thirlwall pointed out, the North still has some toxic masculinity issues that it needs to work out.

British music in general has put many in the Hall of Fame: operatic rock pioneers, Queen; punk rockers the Clash, and the Sex Pistols; and, of course, the group from Liverpool who changed pop history. But it has also filled local pubs with lesser-known bands and singers who've been just as important to individuals and audiences across the country as the groups that became household names. Music is a powerful medium; one that can inspire, alter your mood, or offer comfort and community. Greater Manchester punk band The Fall's 1980 song 'The North will Rise Again' was followed forty years later by Sheffield band Section 60's (which is actually a police stop-and-search law) 'The North will Rise Again', the title re-used to reaffirm commitment to renovation and resilience. And I would argue it did rise again, as we supported one another through a public health crisis in 2020 and emerged to fight for our communities in a post-pandemic era.

Music also reflects the environment in which is created, and Northern music is no exception with its tones of melancholy and anger, or cheekiness and love of a good time. It has provided a soundtrack to many an angsty youth; to hard times and fun times and hours spent wondering what adult life would hold, dreaming of leaving and discovering what else was out there. I wish I could tell my younger self that I would get to learn and experience so much, but that I would end up back where I started, like the protagonist of a parable about finding treasure where you had been all along. Like the same albums you listen to over and over but can still feel moved or find a new meaning in the same lyric you've heard a thousand times, the place I grew up called me back up North to rediscover what I thought I knew.

Back Up North: A Reprise

In days gone by (and some that are not yet past), the North was seen as a world of back-to-back terraced housing and factories, poverty, bad weather and worse accents, and a complicated relationship with the South involving both inferiority and superiority complexes. Most of the back-to-back houses were flattened, and the factories converted into trendy apartment blocks. Accents are also in the process of being lost across the region, and it could be argued that the weather has marginally improved; possibly due to all the smog we churned out of said factories. It also can't be denied that the North's major cities are exciting places to be, even if some Southerners can't stretch the imagination to living as far away from the capital as Manchester, let alone Newcastle.

In being away for so long, I was able to see the region's challenges, curiosities, and treasures with new eyes. From this journey back home, I've learned that there is some kind of umbilical cord connecting you to the land where you grow up and that, even after it's cut, a bond remains – it is, after all, called your 'motherland' for a reason. Whilst identities are always complex and multifaceted, regional identities can be useful constructions that root us in the world. I've been reminded of my privileges compared with my forebearers', and learned to be proud of my family history with its factory workers and firefighters and, I like to think, witches. I've learned that superstition is part of having Lancastrian roots and that I can resist the kind of thinking that tells me I shouldn't believe in magic.

I've learned that the North lives in both a geographical place with its rolling hills north of Shakespeare's hometown and south of Hadrian's Wall; as well as in the psyche, moulded by history, language, and everyday interactions. Although the North-South divide is not what it used to be, it lingers on in the national (sub)conscious. Though a Southern friend of mine argued that "people are people are people", no matter which country, never mind region, let me quote Morrissey in response: "You're southern – you wouldn't understand. When you're northern, you're northern forever, and you're instilled with a certain feel for life that you can't get rid of. You just can't." I agree that there are friendly and cold, or funny and sombre people to be found wherever you go, but both culture and economics are real and have tangible consequences. We can share an English culture whilst recognising a Northern one, in the same way that we can be British yet recognise what both unites and distinguishes English, Scottish, Welsh, and Northern Irish cultures.

Melvyn Bragg's line about Northernness being "a truthful fiction... one of England's great stories," resonates. And meaning is found in stories. While some may argue that we carry a chip on our broad shoulders, we can still take that chip off and dunk it in some gravy while we tell, and re-tell, tales of what it means to be from – and back – up North.

Other Claims to Fame

- In a spate of transportation firsts, the world's first commercial railway was established in Leeds in 1758, the Middleton Colliery Railway; the world's first public railway to use steam locomotives connected collieries near Stockton-on-Tees with County Durham in 1825; and the world's first inter-city railway in the world connected Manchester and Liverpool in 1830.

- The first ever aeroplane flight occurred in Brompton in 1853, with the inventor's hired help at the helm. After a short flight and a prompt crash, the man allegedly climbed out, hobbling off, grumbling: "I was hired to drive not fly."

- The National Trust was founded by a vicar from Cumberland – the "roof of England" – who encouraged Beatrix Potter to write.

- The Angel of the North is one of the biggest statues in England at 20 metres high and 55 metres wide.

- The first keep fit class for housewives was in Sunderland in 1929.

- The M62 is the highest motorway in the UK at 1,221 feet (372 metres). The highest point is located at Windy Hill near Saddleworth Moor in the Peak District. The M6 at Shap Summit in Cumbria also ranks amongst the highest.

- Captain Smith of *RMS Titanic* lived in Waterloo, near Liverpool for 40 years and the eight musicians who played whilst the ship sank were recruited by Liverpudlian music agents.

- The climber George Mallory was from Mobberley in Cheshire. When asked why he wanted to climb Everest, the world's highest mountain, he famously replied: "Because it's there." In 1924 (29 years before Edmund Hillary reached the top) he got near to the summit with his climbing buddy from the Wirral when a snowstorm swept them away, their bodies never to be recovered. In 1995, George's grandson reached the summit in his honour.

- The world's first dog show occurred in Newcastle in 1859. After deciding that showing off your animal property was high entertainment, it shortly followed that the city decided doing the same with their women was a good idea, with Britain's first beauty contest in 1905, called *The Blonde and Brunette Show*.

- Cheshire's Lyme Park stately home was used as Mr Darcy's abode, Pemberley, in the BBC's 1995 TV adaptation of *Pride and Prejudice*.

- 1991's Hollywood blockbuster *Robin Hood: Prince of Thieves* starring Kevin Costner and immortalised by Bryan Adams's 'Everything I Do' soundtrack, featured the iconic Sycamore Gap Tree that stood in a dramatic dip along Hadrian's Wall in Northumberland before it was chopped down in September 2023.

- Although Sherwood Forest belongs to the Midlands, its edges reach up to Sheffield (whose name means 'field boundary' in Old English). Robin is said to be buried in Kirklees after he went to stay with a cousin who he thought was protecting him from the King's men but who, instead, killed him.

References

[1] Pat Mahony & Christine Zmroczek (1997) *Class Matters: 'Working-Class' Women's Perspectives on Social Class.* Taylor & Francis.

[2] Brian Groom (2022) *Northerners: A History, from the Ice Age to the Present Day.* HarperCollins.

[3] BBC (2023) Inside England's second most deprived area, BBC Newsnight.

[4] Alex Niven (2021) Is the Northern Independence party more serious than it looks? *Guardian*. 3 April.

[5] *The Daily Mash* (2020) Birdsong, embroidery and other simply joys that are shit compared to the pub. Digitalbox Ltd. 22 May.

[6] Jini Reddy (2021) *Wanderland: A search for magic in the landscape.* Bloomsbury Publishing.

[7] James Cameron [Dir]. (1997) *Titanic.* Paramount Pictures, USA.

[8] *The Daily Mash* (2020) Northerners delighted to see what scum Southerners really are. Digitalbox Ltd. 26 June.

[9] Larry Elliott (2018) Sun over Blackpool and Scarborough, but dark days are not over. *The Guardian*, 30 June.

[10] Bill Bryson (1990) *Mother Tongue: The Story of the English Language.* Penguin.

[11] Mark Hodkinson (2022) *No One Round Here Reads Tolstoy: Memoirs of a Working-Class Reader,* Canongate.

[12] ITV (2015) *Inside Britain's Food Factories.* Series 1, Episode 2. ITV.

[13] Lancashire Federation of Women's Institute (1920-1980) Lancashire Cook Book.

[14] Words written by Lemn Sissay: lemn@lemnsissay.com

[15] Taylor Heyman (2022) How Vimto stays at the top of the Gulf's Ramadan shopping list. *The National*. April 26.

[16] Panikos Panayi (2010) *Spicing Up Britain: The Multicultural History of British Food.* Reaktion Books.

[17] Reni Eddo-Lodge (2017) *Why I'm No Longer Talking to White People About Race.* Bloomsbury Publishing.

[18] Marina Lewycka, Refugees and Exiles. In: Viet Thanh Nguyen [Ed] (2018) *Displaced: Refugee Writers on Refugee Lives.* Abrams Press. Representation: A M Heath.

[19] Jonathan Pie (2023) Stop the boats. YouTube. 12 August.

[20] R Rao (2017) *Postcolonial Cosmopolitanism: Between home and the World.* University of Oxford.

[21] FH Cheetham (1915-28) *The Church Bells of Lancashire, Transactions of the Lancashire and Cheshire Antiquarian Society.*

[22] Adam Farrer (2023) *Cold Fish Soup,* Saraband books: Glasgow.

[23] Alan Garner (2011) *Collected Folk Tales,* Harper Collins.

[24] Frances Wilson (2013) The A-Z of northern fiction. *The New Statesman.* 5 December.

[25] Richard Smyth (2022) Prospect essay: How northern is the northern novel? [author website]

[26] The God Cast with Fr Alex Frost (2023) Sunder Katwala – How to Be a Patriot. YouTube.

[27] Alan Bennett (2008) *Writing Home,* Faber & Faber.

[28] Quoted in: Richard Smyth (2021) How northern is the northern novel? *Prospect*.

[29] Ben Taylor (2020) Important NHS And Self-Isolation Read, Leeds TV. 3 April. @YorkshireProse

[30] Holly Spanner (n.d.) Why are we so obsessed with true crime? BBC Science Focus.

[31] Mark Herman [Dir.] (1996) *Brassed Off.* Film4 Productions.

[32] Patrick Scott (2014) The stats prove it: The Smiths among most miserable bands ever. *Manchester Evening News*, 31 October.

[33] Joanna Morris (2017) Women 'can't sing rock': Doctor Brown's in Middlesbrough bans female-fronted bands, *Northern Echo*. 11 December.

Investigate our other titles and
stay up to date with all our latest releases at
www.scratchingshedpublishing.co.uk